DREAM CARS

Jean-Rodolphe Piccard

DREAM CARS

Translated from the French by Ian Norris

CRESCENT BOOKS

New York

This 1984 edition is published by Crescent Books,
distributed by Crown Publishers, Inc.

Printed in Italy and bound in Switzerland

Library of Congress Cataloging in Publication Data

Piccard, Jean-Rodolphe.
    Dream Cars.

    "Originally published as The automobile year book of
dream cars, 1981."—Verso t.p.
    Translation of: Grand livre des voitures de rêve.
    1. Automobiles—Miscellanea. I. Title.
TL154.P5313 1983   629.2'222   83-15246
ISBN 0-517-427990

h g f e d c b a

Foreword

I believe the phrase 'Dream Cars' came from the cars of the Motorama Shows which General Motors held each year. It was their own show of specialized cars, and was Harley Earl's inspiration. He wanted cars shown to the public which would be entirely different from the cars they could see in the manufacturer's and dealer's showrooms.

He had a two-fold reason for these attractively different cars. Reason number one was to give the public a thrill by showing them exciting new models, new silhouettes, new grilles, new tail treatments, new interiors, etc. The other reason, the main one, was to wake up the manufacturers and corporate managers to what could be done without meetings and committees, which ultimately boiled a good design down into mediocracy.

Of course, Harley Earl was like my father. I started to work for him when I was twenty-three years old and throughout my career I have followed in his footsteps. I can safely say that my philosophy is exactly the same as his would have been.

After seeing these shows, the public would write in and request that a certain model be made, and many times management would be awakened to the fact that there was a demand for this car. The Corvette is a good example. Without show cars (dream cars) there is no 'show'. In each Motorama, or the automobile shows of Paris, London, Geneva, and New York, the writers would look for an exciting good design.

For the show cars of the future there is a great need for a return to elegance. Cars of the '30s had refinement, and all of this is more important today with cars becoming smaller and more frugal. If the motor industry continues to make ugly little hare-lipped frogs, the day of the motor car appealing to the personal pride of ownership will be over. A motor car must be more than just transportation.

Can it be that automobile design, modern automobile design, is to be like some modern music—harsh, loud and ugly?

Many of the modern designs are crude contortions created by the same men that created the classics of a few years ago. Certainly Giugiaro must realize his Maserati Ghibli is a classic compared to the cars he is doing today.

The average motor car viewer is anxious to see something new, not just new in the sense of shock value, but to see something that is beautiful.

The Turin Automobile Show has been the home of the greatest body designers in the world, and to me it is the most exciting show. It is where I always wanted to show my latest creations, such as the Sting Ray, the Manta Ray or the Monzas. I also felt the Geneva Show was one of the greatest shows, and I was very pleased to show the Seville Elegante there.

Show cars are designers' cars, not committee cars. We need these cars to show the direction of style to come. It saddens me to see some of the designs today, squared-off ugly boxes as compared with the flowing lines of the cars of twenty years ago. The present designers and even the great names like Bertone, Giugiaro and Pininfarina have become entranced with a Picasso-like direction.

I am writing this in my studio in Palm Beach, Florida, where I am surrounded by beautiful illustrations by Walter Gotschke, Peter Helck, Brian de Grineau, Michael Turner and Melborne Brindle. These artists have also done beautiful illustrations of race cars in the late '20s. It's difficult to believe, but I think the present racing cars are even uglier than the passenger cars.

I sincerely hope the trend will soon return to elegance.

I'm sorry to get so turned-on emotionally about these ugly trends, but that is the way I feel.

Thank God I can surround myself in my studio with the beautiful cars of the past and pray they will return.

January 1980

William L. Mitchell

PAUL BRACQ is chief interior stylist at the Peugeot Styling Centre. He studied body design and construction at college and worked with the French stylist Philippe Charbonneaux from 1953 to 1955. He was Director of advanced studies at the Mercedes Benz styling studio from 1957 to 1967, when he went to work with the Brissoneau and Lotz design consultancy. In 1970 he was appointed chief of styling for BMW, a position he held until he moved to Peugeot in 1974.

GIUSEPPE (NUCCIO) BERTONE joined the coach-building firm of Carozzeria Bertone S.p.a., which his father Giovanni had founded in 1912, in 1934 and became responsible for its direction after the war. Among the numerous stylists who have worked under his leadership are Mario Revelli de Beaumont, Franco Scaglione, Giorgio Giugiaro, Giovanni Michelotti, and Marcello Gandini.

WILLIAM M. BROWNLIE is Director — Small Car, International and Advance Design, of the Chrysler Corporation. Born in 1925, he started his career as a stylist with Ford in 1949 and joined the Briggs Manufacturing body-building company as an advanced styling designer in 1952. When the Chrysler Corporation bought Briggs in 1953 he became Manager of Exterior styling for the parent company. In 1961 he was appointed chief stylist for the Dodge Lancer Styling Studio and in 1968 was promoted to the position of Executive Stylist for Dodge cars and trucks. He moved to the company's Small Car design activities in 1970 and has worked in this area since then, with steadily increasing responsibilities which culminated in his appointment to his present position in 1978.

GIORGIO GIUGIARO is a director of the Ital Design consultancy which he founded in 1968 with Aldo Mantovani and Luciano Bosio. Recruited to the Fiat styling studio by Dante Giacosa when he was 17, he worked with the company for four years before moving to Bertone. He stayed there for five years and worked on a number of production car designs as well prototypes. In 1965, at the age of only 27, he was recruited as Head of Projects and Style for Ghia. After only a year he decided to work on his own, but Ghia retained him as a consultant until he took the decision to set up Ital Design with his partners.

What are dream cars?

How did they originate and evolve into their present state? What is their future? To find out the answers to these questions and to learn something of the minds that create those dream cars, we asked the same set of questions to eight men, each one a leader in the world of automobile styling and each one with a long experience in the business of creating not only the mass-production cars which are an integral part of our lives, but also the trend-setting cars which so often, in probing the outer limits of style, form the ideas for the production cars of tomorrow or the day after. We asked each of these men the same questions and their answers form the principal chapters of this book. Sometimes they are contradictory but that is because they are creative people, and creative people are essentially individualists, and it can be seen from the examples of their work in the book how that individuality shows itself as a personal design style.

FILIPPO SAPINO is Vice President and Managing Director of Ghia, the Ford Motor Company's European styling 'think-tank'. Born in Turin, he attended the city's Technical Institute after becoming a car enthusiast at the age of ten. When he left the Institute in 1959 he went to work at the Ghia studio and remained with the firm until 1967, when he left to join Pininfarina. In 1969 Ford decided to set up its own design studio in Turin and Mr Sapino was chosen to be its head. In 1973 Ghia became a Ford subsiduary and he moved back to his former employers, but this time as top man in the operation.

SERGIO PININFARINA has been the President of the company which his father, Battista Pininfarina, founded in 1930, since 1966. With his brother-in-law, Renzo Carli, he took over the running of the company in 1958 when his father went into semi-retirement. Among the designers who have worked under his direction are Tom Tjaarda, Filippo Sapino, Paolo Martin, Francesco Martinengo and Leonardo Fioravanti.

IRVIN W. RYBICKI has been Vice President in charge of the Design Staff of General Motors since 1977. After showing an enthusiasm for car design whilst still at school, he joined the GM Styling department in 1945. He progressed through the department and was made Oldsmobile chief designer in 1957. In 1962 he was appointed as Chevrolet chief designer and three years later became responsible for the GMC truck studios in addition to the Chevrolet car studios. Pontiac cars and Chevrolet trucks were added to his responsibilities in 1970 and in 1972 he was named as executive in charge of Oldsmobile, Buick, and Cadillac passenger cars, a post he held until moving to his present position. He played a major part in the massive re-design programme which GM carried out at the end of the 'seventies.

ROBERT F. ZOKAS is Director of Ford Motor Company's North American Small Car and Truck Design Office. With a background and training in fine art, he joined Ford in 1955 as an illustrator in what was then called the Styling Office. After work on styling for Edsel, Lincoln-Mercury and Ford, he was appointed Corporate Design Manager, with responsibility for corporate identity, in 1965. He returned to the design operation in 1968, working on interior trim design. He worked on a wide variety of interior design projects on all types of vehicles until 1976 when he was named as Director of the Light Car Design Office, responsible for the design and development of all North American small cars. In 1978 he was put in charge of the design and development of all Ford's international and advanced concepts, including vehicles produced by Ghia. He was appointed to his present position in 1979.

What is a dream car?

GIORGIO GIUGIARO — ITAL DESIGN   I prefer the term 'show car' to 'Dream Car', and I think that all such cars are partly public relations exercises to promote the image of their constructors and partly experimental vehicles which explore new developments in styling trends and techniques. There are some vehicles which are primarily experimental and which serve as test-beds for new styling ideas, mechanical developments, materials, or any combination of these elements. There are, on the other hand, a few cars which are built purely as publicity vehicles, with little in the way of technical innovation.

FILIPPO SAPINO — GHIA   I would say that the simple definition of the term 'dream car' would be the pure realisation, in terms of a car, of human imagination and enthusiasm expressed in its most free form. But the line between a 'dream car' and a 'show car' is unclear and more difficult to define. Perhaps show cars are the dream cars of today, because the term 'dream car' has come to have a derogatory air about it in the past few years, being used to describe projects which are detached from real life. I consider the real dream cars were those built up to about 1964 and which belonged to an era when the main purpose of the specially-built car was to catch the public's imagination, and the considerations of practicality and function which must be present in a serious project were of a secondary nature.

In my opinion, today's dream car or show car still retains the element of bravura on the part of the designer and coachbuilder which will stir the feelings of the everyday motorist, but it is constructed on a much more realistic basis than before. Today the designer must exercise a degree of self-control in restraining his imagination. He can allow it a certain amount of freedom, but it must not go beyond the bounds of practicality and function which must govern a realistic experimental vehicle. There are even stronger constraints on the imagination of a stylist engaged on a design prototype. In this case, the stylist's creativity is severely restricted by the jungle of regulations of all types which govern the design of a production car today.

I would liken the stylist's job in designing these three types of vehicle to that of attacking a speed record on a bicycle. Designing a dream car is like doing the run on a racing cycle, a show car design is like trying it on a touring machine, and creating a design prototype is the equivalent to trying it on a baker's delivery bike.

SERGIO PININFARINA   A dream car is a car that makes one dream. In general, the term 'dream car' can be applied to two types of car. Firstly, there is that class of car which because of their luxurious style, their sporting character, the reputation which their constructors—such as Ferrari and Rolls-Royce—enjoy, and their high price—represent a kind of dream which is for the greater part of the population unattainable. The second type of dream cars are those which are designed and built as pure exercises in style, without the constraints imposed on production cars by considerations of cost or ease of production.

R.F. ZOKAS — FORD   A dream car is a car which best represents the designer's interpretation of the future including unusual operating features, mechanical components and the unique application of materials.

9

IRVIN W. RYBICKI — GENERAL MOTORS   Dream Cars, Show Cars, and Design Prototypes are all interesting words that may bring quite different images to mind as different people perceive them. Let me give you my views of the three types:

Dream Cars were cars designed during the post-World War II era embodying designers' ideas of what the public might want to have once production got going. They were usually non-operating full-size models of cars that would draw plenty of attention when brought into any public place. They embodied new ideas in vehicle configuration, body form, and detail styling items.

Show Cars are similar to dream cars (in some people's language they are the same) but I think they tend to be less extravagant. They are usually modified versions of cars already on the market. The modifications are usually in the field of details such as grille textures, roof surfaces, and paint and trim combinations.

Design Prototypes are specific vehicles which are shown to corporate management by the design staff for approval as the final step before release of the design information to the divisions that will manufacture them. They are, consequently, highly secret models which are not shown to the public, but rather serve as internal decision-making tools and may be used for the development of advertising photography before their 'replica' reaches production.

NUCCIO BERTONE   One could write a great deal about dream cars. I shall ignore those vehicles built purely for display, for the reason that they do not represent a serious endeavour. Let us consider instead those models which, although they do not have the benefit of an experimental phase before production, do represent real, driveable, cars. Such prototypes vary considerably in their conception and their aims, but they all put forward new concepts which are there for the consideration of the public and of other designers and manufacturers as sign-posts to future thinking. Usually, their form stimulates the public's imagination and appeals to the sense of beauty and individuality which each of us has in him. We find in such a car the realisation of a dream which is present in us all, but which only the artist has the ability to translate into a concrete form. One can almost talk of 'industrial art' in this context. In the case of prototypes the stylist can dare to use construction techniques and solutions which could never be used in a production vehicle, but such daring can act as the stimulus to a process of experimentation and development which may devise practical methods of realising something which started as just a stylist's dream.

PAUL BRACQ   The dream car is the realisation of how a manufacturer or coachbuilder sees their own 'brand image' projected into the future. It is usually a single vehicle which is shown at international automobile shows to give the public the opportunity to see the manufacturer's ideas of future developments in the fields of styling, technical innovation, and safety. A dream car should not in any way resemble the company's current production vehicles or future projects planned for production, because that could adversely affect the sales of the current models. The introduction of a dream car can be a double-edged weapon. On the positive side, it is an excellent means of showing the public and the press the dynamic qualities of the company's design and research staff in terms of styling and technology, and it is useful in that it enables public reaction to new styling and marketing trends to be gauged. On the negative side there is the possibility of letting competing companies know the lines along which the manufacturer's design staff are proceeding, and it is difficult to find a theme for a dream car which will not interfere with a major manufacturer's new model programme, which is committed to replacing the range every eight to ten years. For the great coachbuilders, there is no negative side to the production of dream cars—on the contrary, they provide an excellent means of bringing their work to the notice of the public, the press, and the major manufacturers. In my opinion, there are three types of dream cars. The first is the classification of dream cars as 'idea cars', or vehicles which give an indication of future models from the marque—for example the Buick Y-Job of 1938 was ten years ahead of the production cars of its time. The collaboration between Chrysler and Ghia gave birth to a whole series of idea cars which themselves influenced the company's production cars—good examples of this were the Flight Sweep II and Falcon I of 1957. In that same year, two years after they had introduced the dream car of the same name, Cadillac introduced the production model of the Eldorado Brougham at the New York Show. It was a Pininfarina prototype, the Florida II, which was made into the Lancia Flaminia of 1958. Talking of Pininfarina, one has to mention his Sigma of 1964 which was the first of the safety cars. The second classification is dream cars as 'show cars'. In this group I would place all those cars which have been produced purely in order to draw people to a motor show stand. It is difficult to classify them because even an expert has difficulty in distinguishing between the many 'display vehicles', 'experimental cars', and the many turbine cars which have been produced. As an example, I would quote the first GM turbine car, the 1954 Firebird, which was closer to aircraft than automobile design and which was overloaded with unnecessary flourishes and visual references to contemporary fighter planes like the Douglas Skyray. Unlike the true experimental car, where new technology is not necessarily evident from the styling, the show car is designed to impress the public, who are always more impressed by outward appearances than hidden engineering progress. Some of these cars were pure mock-ups; an expression of the stylist's ideas which had no limit placed on them by industrial or commercial realities.

The third group is the dream car as a competition car; all competition cars represent an area inaccessible to the general public except in dreams.

WILLIAM M. BROWNLIE — CHRYSLER CORPORATION I think that dream cars are generally considered by the general public as something that is extremely far out in concept—almost to the extent of something like a car without wheels or something that might fly. A show car I consider as something that is much closer to us, perhaps only five or ten years away, and still recogniseable as an automobile; something that the customer can see himself driving in the not-too-distant future. I see show cars and dream cars as two very different categories. I think that our 'Norseman'—which was never shown because it sank in the *Andrea Doria*—was an example of a true dream car because it had many design and engineering concepts which were totally new and fresh. Show cars, on the other hand, project up to about five years hence. There are many examples from Ford, GM, and ourselves that make the round of the shows and are regarded as marketing exercises and examples of what people will or will not like. Finally, I'd class a design prototype as something we were going to build tomorrow.

11

What is the purpose of the dream car?

IRVIN W. RYBICKI — GENERAL MOTORS Dream cars have several purposes: they act as stimulants to the designers who have a chance to express fresh ideas, they serve as public relations attractions that draw spectators to car shows and exhibits, and they can serve to measure the public's like or dislike of the ideas proposed.

R.F. ZOKAS — FORD Dream cars force the designer to project his thinking into the future and to excite the public, thus creating interest in the company and its products.

NUCCIO BERTONE There are innumerable reasons for the existence of dream cars. They can serve as pure research vehicles, unrestrained by the constraints of production requirements or legislation. Such research will often reveal avenues for exploration which will result in new ideas applicable to the everyday car. There are also commercial considerations which make it necessary to find out the public's acceptance or rejection of new ideas which are under consideration. Finally there is the very important aspect of publicity. A dream car is almost a showpiece which can bring its creators wide exposure in the media and the resulting free publicity is very important.

SERGIO PININFARINA Every automobile manufacturer has a design department which pursues research into the many technical and styling problems which concern their products. The result of these studies are experimental vehicles which can either remain secret or be shown at automobile shows as a means of judging the public's reaction.

FILIPPO SAPINO — GHIA The reasons for building the dream cars of yesterday and the show cars of today and tomorrow have been, and always will be, the same. Apart from acting as a barometer of the public's taste, their value is that they give their designers the opportunity to follow a path of development which reaches far into the future and which will serve as a reference for future passenger car designs. Certainly, only the most practical elements will be applied to production cars, but the way-out ideas which are tried and rejected are just as useful because they tell us in advance, at minimum cost, those solutions which are not worth following up.

GIORGIO GIUGIARO — ITAL DESIGN That is an easy question for me to answer because I often have to use my earlier prototypes as examples when persuading our clients to use certain details in production vehicles. I'm talking about such things as window-lift mechanisms, air-intakes, spoilers, gutters, lamps, windscreens and interior furnishings for example.

PAUL BRACQ Dream cars were important weapons in the desperate struggles between the American car companies in the 'fifties, and in the 'sixties served the same purpose in the battle between the Italian coachbuilders which was fought out in the great international automobile shows.

WILLIAM M. BROWNLIE — CHRYSLER CORPORATION From the designer's viewpoint, he is looking for new aesthetic ideas in creating a dream car, but from the company's viewpoint they are trying to find out what kind of market appeal the dream car might have and to follow-up on popular styling trends as a means of improving sales. To return to the designer's view of things, I think that one can compare the automobile designer's task with that of a surgeon in that if the surgeon's knife is out of line by a sixteenth of an inch, the patient is dead; if the stylist's pencil is a sixteenth of an inch out, the design is an ugly one instead of a thing of beauty. All the time, the designer is trying to put together that combination of lines and forms which will make a beautiful car. And that's why show cars and dream cars are developed; trying to find that new form, trying to marry all the geometric forms in such a manner that suddenly, lo and behold, the highlights which we see—which are really the line—are so pleasing, so new, so self-expressing that you walk away enthused and happy, and almost willing to buy. That's the reason really.

What they think…

Experimental cars are libraries for hot ideas. It's important to have cars made up full-size so our people can see them in true perspective.

George W. Walker, Ford Vice-President in charge of styling, 1956.

The idea of the experimental car was to test new styling and engineering ideas in a complete, new car… The reactions of the hundreds of thousands of viewers to these so called 'dream cars' showed that the public wanted and was ready to accept more daring steps in styling and engineering.

Alfred P. Sloan Jr., Board Chairman of General Motors 1937-1955.

There was a time when we in General Motors styling felt we had to hold back on some of our design ideas because the public wasn't ready for them yet. In the showing of dream cars about the nation, however, we learned that the public's thinking in automobile design was ahead of ours, not behind. More than 2 million persons see our experimental cars each year in the Motorama alone. They talk about them, they say what they like—and what they don't like. And we listen, very carefully.

Harley J. Earl, Vice-President in charge of styling, General Motors, 1956.

Every car we've built has been runnable and produceable, with one exception. We don't believe in the Buck Rogerish, splash type dream car. Our way of doing it has limited us in some ways, but we think it's more practical even though our models cost more than the mock-up, pure show car.

Virgil M. Exner, Director of Styling, Chrysler Corporation, 1956.

These so-called dream cars aren't as futuristic as they look. Stick around for a year or two and we'll prove it.

George W. Walker, Ford Vice-President in charge of styling, 1956.

13

Is a dream car the work of one man?

IRVIN W. RYBICKI — GENERAL MOTORS No one designer does all things, yet many individual cars have been the product of small teams. We believe in the importance of the individual personality of our product. There is no doubt that the character in certain cars can be identified with the particular chief designer in whose studios it was executed. I think that one of the differences between mass production cars and show cars is that the mass production car must meet many requirements from component interchangeability to Federal Safety Standards while the experimental car can be much freer in its expression. There is quite a difference between a fifty thousand dollar Ferrari that is custom-built for one man and a five thousand dollar Buick that must be manufactured on tools whose cost is amortised in a production run of a quarter of a million units!

R.F. ZOKAS — FORD Not entirely true, many dream cars are created through team effort. The input from many designers as well as engineers.

NUCCIO BERTONE It is usually so, even if—as frequently happens—two different stylists are responsible for solving the differing problems presented by the interior and exterior treatment of the car. In other cases, the concept and outline of the direction which the design should follow are chosen by someone else. Often the stylist is the sole interpreter and executor on the behalf of another person, whose original idea the designer is interpreting. It is therefore often difficult to trace back to one single person the conception of a prototype.

FILIPPO SAPINO — GHIA Many dream cars are the result of the creative efforts of a single stylist, but many others are the result of the work of a team. You must never forget the contribution made to the successful completion of a project by the technicians and car builders—particularly in the case of working prototypes which are so complex.

GIORGIO GIUGIARO — ITAL DESIGN It is not true. You can create a dream car with a team in the same way that music can be composed, or a novel written, by two people in collaboration. When I was working with Bertone, I worked in the closest collaboration with the body-builder.

SERGIO PININFARINA I don't believe that you could say that in every case; it is certainly not true in our organisation.

PAUL BRACQ In an orchestra, only the conductor's name is quoted, not those of all the members, and it is the same thing for the team which works together to produce a dream car. It often represents the philosophy of the head of the design studio who will be responsible for the original styling drawings.

WILLIAM M. BROWNLIE — CHRYSLER CORPORATION There are many dream cars which have come from the seed of one person's idea, an idea which has been translated directly into a car and been great. However, there are many other times that the dreams or ideas come from one person and have then been communicated to another designer, and because of the interchange between two very talented people, that idea has been nurtured to the point where it has blossomed into something even better. Because of that, I would suggest that an idea or a dream does not always come from only one person. There are times when it has to be helped by another person or persons through discussion, communication, and analysis to the point where it becomes a team effort.

14

What are the steps in the design and construction of a dream car?

NUCCIO BERTONE The progression is very simple. First of all there is the decision-making stage, where the theme to be followed is decided upon, then the preparation of the detailed constructional drawings, the manufacture of the body-stamping tools followed by the various components of the car, and finally the assembly of the components.

FILIPPO SAPINO — GHIA There is hardly any difference—at least for the coachbuilder—between the phases in the development of a dream car and those of a prototype for a production car. Sketches are made, and a choice is made from a selection of these. A scale model is then made and full-scale drawings prepared so that a full-size mock-up can be produced in plaster, wood or fibreglass. After this point there are differences because a dream car will usually employ unusual and sophisticated features in its design. It will therefore require more detailed design work on its technical aspects and a greater degree of experimentation in the workshop than a normal prototype would. After this phase there are all the normal steps in the production process: stamping out the panels, assembly, revision and modification, painting, trimming, and testing.

GIORGIO GIUGIARO — ITAL DESIGN At Ital Design, the main characteristic of the production of a dream car is that of speed of execution. Since there is no client to convince, I lay out the design of the car in a simplified form and then make the arrangements for the construction of a model without wasting time. From a conceptual point of view, I don't design a prototype with a particular show in view. The car takes shape in my mind over a period of time; I 'design' it mentally over as long a period as is necessary for it to reach a stage where it is a completely-formed concept.

IRVIN W. RYBICKI — GENERAL MOTORS With us, the stages are engineering layout, structural analysis, parts fabrication, and final assembly and paint.

R.F. ZOKAS — FORD The procedure is as follows: Rough sketches, design selection, full-size drawings and renderings, full-size clay model, fibreglass cast, chassis construction or modification, steel body build, paint, interior fabrication and installation.

PAUL BRACQ The building of a dream car is essentially a work of craftsmanship.

WILLIAM M. BROWNLIE — CHRYSLER CORPORATION There are many steps, and they are the same wherever the car is produced but I feel that the active participation and control of the designer himself is important. After a decision has been reached to go ahead on a particular design and a model is being produced, the designer who came up with the idea initially supervises the building of the model to make sure that the end result is exactly what he was thinking about. So he is assisting, and in many cases providing additional material, to make sure that in the creation of the actual car the sculptor or panel-beater is forming the car in the correct way.
In the days when we first collaborated with Ghia, we simply sent them a single sketch, with no mechanical drawings or other material. Ghia would interpret the sketch and we would go over to Turin to see the vehicle, already started in metal, to see if they had captured the essence of the sketch. In most cases they really had.

Some time soon—and I'm optimistic about it—the motor car will exist in only two forms: sensible everyday transportation and sport—with little relation between the two. The sumptuous display of riches on wheels will have had its day, for better or worse. But the anachronistic dream cars will remain, to be exhumed by future archaeologists throughout eternity, and identified as the most beautiful and the most aberrant of all our artifacts, of all time.

Jean-Francis Held   Automobile Year N° 20, 1972-1973

1939 — Buick Y-Job This fore-runner of all the American Dream Cars was created in 1939 by Harley Earl, director of the GM styling studio, in collaboration with George Snyder, and was presented to the press and public a year later. It was a two-seat roadster based on a lengthened Buick Super chassis, and was extremely low-slung for its day, despite the fact that its in-line 8 cylinder engine dictated a relatively high bonnet-line. Its lines influenced the styling of post-war cars and certain details, particularly the grille and badge design, remained in use on Buick models up to 1958. The top folded electrically into a compartment in the boot and the wing-mounted headlamps were retractable. Harley Earl used the car as his personal transport between 1942 and 1944. Three years later the car was unfortunately modified to accept headlamps and bumpers from a production vehicle and it is in this form that it is now on view in the Alfred P. Sloan Jr. Museum in Flint, Michigan.

1933 — Cadillac Aerodynamic Coupé This could be considered as the American automobile industry's first 'Show Car'. It was built for the Chicago World's Fair in 1933 and was the main exhibit in the General Motors Pavillon. As a reaction against the angular styles which were currently in vogue, the young stylists working under the direction of Harley Earl gave it a completely new line with the boot and spare wheel completely integrated, hidden in the sweeping rear end.

1941 — Chrysler Thunderbolt The Thunderbolt was to Chrysler what the Y-Job was to GM. This first Chrysler experimental model was designed by Le Baron and was unusual in that six examples were made for exhibition by dealers. A two-door coupé, it had a top which retracted into the boot at the press of a button. Similarly, the retractable headlights, electric windows, and door-locks were also push-button controlled.

1936 — Lancia Aprilia It is impossible to avoid comparisons between the Thunderbolt and this aerodynamically styled Lancia Aprilia. Both have the same streamlining and faired-in wings, but whilst the Buick was destined for display in dealer showrooms, the Pininfarina Lancia was run as a high-performance prototype in record attempts and hill-climbs.

19

1951 — Buick XP-300 Many of GM's dream cars were revolutionary only in appearance, but this was not the case with the XP-300, which was an experimental car in every aspect. Four years were needed for Charles Chayne, Buick's chief engineer, to bring the project to fruition. The car made its first appearance in an unfinished form at the 1951 Chicago Auto Show, where its long (16 feet overall) monocoque body was found to hide a number of technical novelties beneath its crowd-pleasing contours. Notable points of the specification were a de Dion rear axle, doors with steel

reinforcing bars which locked hydraulically into place as they closed, a 3.5 litre V8 with a Roots type supercharger which burned petrol (gasoline) below 2500 rpm and methanol at higher speeds, a rear-mounted modified Dynaflow transmission, inboard rear brakes, four hydraulic jacks, a reversing lamp in the rear 'jet outlet', a boot (trunk) with twin lids hinged at the centre-line, hydraulically-adjustable seats, and electric windows. Weighing 3141 lbs, the car could accelerate from 0 to 60 mph in 8 seconds, thanks to its 335 hp produced by the mixed fuel engine.

1951 — Buick Le Sabre Mechanically similar to the XP-300, the incredible Le Sabre was styled by Harley Earl (above) with lines influenced by the then-new jet fighter planes. The car was remarkable for its unusual headlamp treatment — the grille in the central 'snout' rotated to reveal a single central pair of lights. The long rear fins flowed into the rear bumper and housed not only the rear lights, but also the exhaust outlets. Flaps in the rear quarters opened to reveal fillers for the twin fuel cells; petrol on the left and methanol on the right. A car which influenced stylists and customisers for years after, the Le Sabre bristled with advanced and unusual engineering and styling ideas. Among them were the use of cast magnesium for most of the body panels, the hood, which was completely concealed beneath the rear decking and rose into position automatically if rain fell on a sensitive panel on the transmission tunnel between the front seats, and the seats themselves, which had heated panels — anticipating contemporary Swedish designs by some 25 years! In the space of a few months, the Le Sabre became an automotive star, drawing crowds wherever it was shown.

The Le Sabre influenced a whole generation of stylists in Europe as well as the United States. Sometimes the results looked more like copying than influence as, for instance, in the case of this Salmson photographed in 1953 at a Paris concours d'elegance.

23

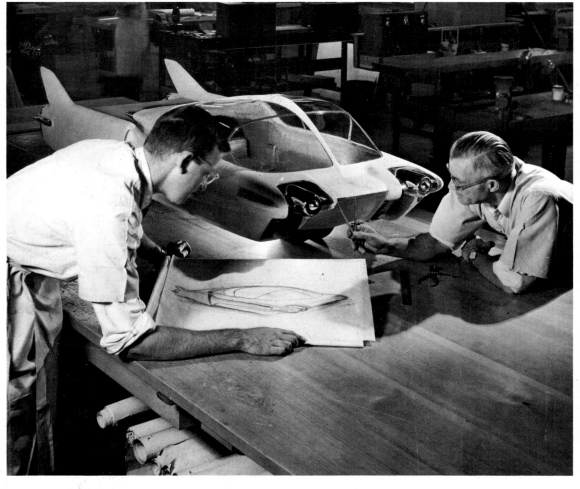

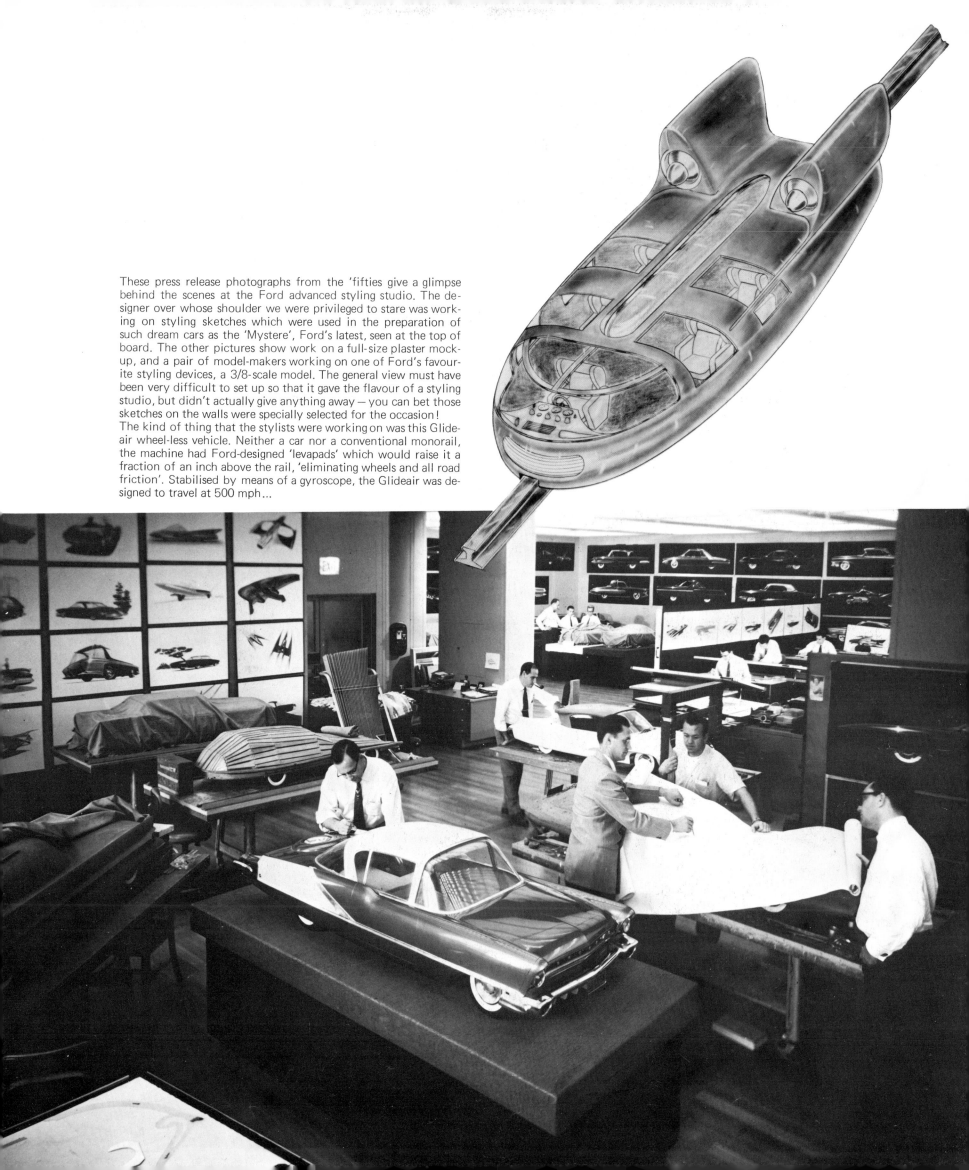

These press release photographs from the 'fifties give a glimpse behind the scenes at the Ford advanced styling studio. The designer over whose shoulder we were privileged to stare was working on styling sketches which were used in the preparation of such dream cars as the 'Mystere', Ford's latest, seen at the top of board. The other pictures show work on a full-size plaster mock-up, and a pair of model-makers working on one of Ford's favourite styling devices, a 3/8-scale model. The general view must have been very difficult to set up so that it gave the flavour of a styling studio, but didn't actually give anything away — you can bet those sketches on the walls were specially selected for the occasion!

The kind of thing that the stylists were working on was this Glideair wheel-less vehicle. Neither a car nor a conventional monorail, the machine had Ford-designed 'levapads' which would raise it a fraction of an inch above the rail, 'eliminating wheels and all road friction'. Stabilised by means of a gyroscope, the Glideair was designed to travel at 500 mph...

1951 — Plymouth XX-500 The work of Mario Boano and Luigi Segre, this car marked the start of a long collaboration between Chrysler and Ghia. The proposal to build the car was put to Chrysler by the Turin firm as a way of showing its capabilities in the field of special bodies. The American firm were happy with the result and this led to Chrysler president K.T. Keller giving Virgil M. Exner, in charge of styling at the company since 1949, the go-ahead to produce what was to become a whole series of 'idea cars'.

1951 — Chrysler K-310 The 'K' in the designation of this five-place sports coupé was in honour of Chrysler's president. Ghia fabricated the steel body, working from a 3/8-scale model and building on a V8 Saratoga chassis. Originally, the spare wheel was visible, but it was later moved to a resting place in the boot floor — but not without leaving traces of its previous position in the boot-lid shape. This styling motif was to re-appear on later production models from the company, together with the egg-box grille and the prismatic rear lamps.

26

1952 — Lancia Aurelia PF 200 Pininfarina was another stylist who was influenced by the aircraft theme, but his PF 200 models were designed with visual appeal as much in mind as aerodynamics. The coupé, like the convertible, had a nozzle-type air-intake with a rounded shape and the aircraft influence also showed in the wind-screen, roof, and rear window, which combined to resemble a fighter cockpit.

1952 — Chrysler SS Following the K-310 and the convertible version of the C-200, Virgil M. Exner had Ghia make two Chrysler 'Styling Specials' at the request of C.B. Thomas, the director of the company's export sales department. The fast-back model (below) was a three-place coupé on a shortened New Yorker chassis and made its debut at the Paris Show in 1952.

1953-1954 — Dodge Firearrow I and II The Dodge Firearrow roadster, first shown as a full-size mock-up (left) was one of the third series of experimental cars designed by Virgil M. Exner at Chrysler and built by Ghia in Turin. The prototype was distinguished from the final version (above) by its twin headlamps, full wheel-discs, and the metallic grey moulding which encircled its bright red body. The seats were upholstered in yellow-buff leather with maroon piping. The Firearrow II was almost identical apart from a few modifications which included a re-designed moulding, which now finished at the head and tail lamps, and a new grille with a heavy transverse bar which served as a bumper. The second car was finished in pale yellow and had a black moulding. Instead of a single boot, the car had separate housings for the spare wheel and luggage, the latter being situated directly behind the black leather-trimmed seats.

1954 — Dodge Firearrow Sport Coupé After the roadster, the coupé. A re-thought front-end featured a concave grille, a return to twin headlamps, and the reduction of the bumpers to a pair of chromed bananas. The coupé's smooth looks had an aerodynamic, as well as visual, appeal — the car was timed at over 135 miles per hour.

1954 — Dodge Firearrow Convertible The Firearrow series came to an end in late 1954 with a four-seat convertible very similar in style to the coupé. The only differences were the grille, with a less rounded shape and rectangular grid formation, and an interior trimmed in a black and white diamond pattern. This was the car on which the Dual-Ghia, produced in very small numbers by the Dual company of Detroit, was based.

1953 — Cadillac Orleans Chrome by the bucket-full decorates the maw of this Cadillac, which one feels would hold as much interest for students of Freudian symbolism as it would for those of automobile styling. The post-war euphoria of the American motor industry and the concept of conspicuous consumption was never better expressed than in this car — incidentally the first American vehicle with pillarless construction.

1953 — Pontiac Parisienne Dream cars do not always have to look to the future, the past can also be a source of inspiration. For this show car, aptly christened the Parisienne, the company's stylists chose to copy a style which was one of the most popular in the catalogues of coachbuilders between the wars — the coupé de ville.

1953 — Cadillac Le Mans Did visitors to the GM Motorama in 1953 realise that the Le Mans was a foretaste of the cars which Cadillac would offer for sale from 1954 to 1956 ? The answer is probably yes, for many of the styling features, such as hooded headlamps, bomb-shaped over-riders, an 'egg-box' grille, a wrap-round windscreen, tailfins, and rearlights in the rear wings, had already been made available on a limited production model, the Eldorado convertible.

1953-1955 — BAT BAT in this case refers to 'Berlina Aero-Tecnica' but there is something of the flying mammal in its combination of wings and sharp nose. Using an Alfa Romeo 1900 chassis as a base, Bertone and the stylist Scaglione created a prototype which, in the course of its development through three versions (numbered 5, 7, and 9) combined exciting looks with technical progress. The combination of sloping glass areas, faired-in wheels, and the curved wings funnelling the airflow over a long tail gave the car an impressively low drag factor for its day (0.9) and a top speed of 125 mph.

1954 — De Soto Adventurer I This car, designed in 1954 by Virgil M. Exner, brought to an end the series of Chrysler experimental cars which started in 1951 with the K-310. It offered space for four passengers but had minimal overall dimensions, thanks to the almost complete absence of overhang front and rear which kept the length down to 15 ft 7 ins. Exner considered it one of his favourite designs and used it as his personal car for three years. If it had entered production it would have been the first American 2 + 2 coupé on the market.

1954 — De Soto Adventurer II The ▷ Adventurer I had an Italian air about it, although it had been designed by an American. The Adventurer II, on the other hand, was entirely built and designed in Italy by Ghia and looked American. Another paradox was that despite its generous exterior dimensions (it was larger than its predecessor) it was only a two-seater. The tinted plastic rear window retracted electrically into the boot at the touch of a button.

1954 — Plymouth Explorer Very similar to the Dodge Firearrow coupé, the Explorer was distinguishable by such details as the horizontal bumpers, exhaust pipes combined in the rearlamp cluster, single headlights, and a side moulding with the parking lights built in to it. The car was finished in bright green with the side moulding picked out in white enamel. The upholstery was in white leather with black 'accents'.

1954 — Packard Panther A hotch-potch of different styling tendencies: overhanging headlamp cowls which run over to form a lip which surmonts the entire front end and runs back along the wing, a rounded grille traversed by the bumper and its attendant 'bomb' over-riders. However, by comparison with Packard's contemporary production models, the Panther was positively restrained.

1954 — Plymouth Belmont This car was built for Chrysler's Plymouth division by the Briggs Manufacturing Company and used a 1954 Dodge chassis with a 3.9 litre V8 engine. The metallic blue body was constructed in reinforced fibreglass, so from a technical point of view the exercise was probably worthwhile. Its aesthetic value is less certain.

1955 — Dodge Granada 'The first one-piece, all-plastic-body car ever developed by the auto industry on a conventional chassis' said the press release of the time, adding that: 'Even the bumpers, structural members, and body-attaching brackets are made of fibreglass'. No comment.

36

1954 — Ford FX-Atmos This is the car which introduced visitors to the 1954 Chicago Auto Show to styling ideas 'so advanced that they formerly had been seen only in Ford styling studios'. According to L.D. Crusoe, General Manager of the Ford Division and a vice-president of the Ford Motor Company, the car 'represents one of many avenues which styling could take in the future.' The plastic body was patriotically finished in the American colours: red for the bands on the bonnet and rear wings, blue for the rear deck, and white for the rest.

1955 — Lincoln Futura Setting aside the idea of a presentation in a hotel or country club, far from the eyes of the general public, Ford held the introduction party in New York's Central Park. The car was driven there through the downtown traffic, gliding through the jams like a barracuda passing through a gathering of whales, and leaving even thicker jams wherever it had passed as the drivers of more mundane vehicles stopped to stare. Designed by Lincoln-Mercury stylists and built by Ghia, its interior furnishing were as futuristic as its body. The petrol gauge, oil-pressure and water temperature warning lights, speedometer, and tachometer were set in the centre of the two-branched steering wheel, and other secondary controls were grouped along the fascia panel with sliding covers for when they were not in use. The circular radio aerial contained a microphone which captured and amplified the sounds of traffic approaching from the rear and the centre section of the roof swung up when the doors were opened.

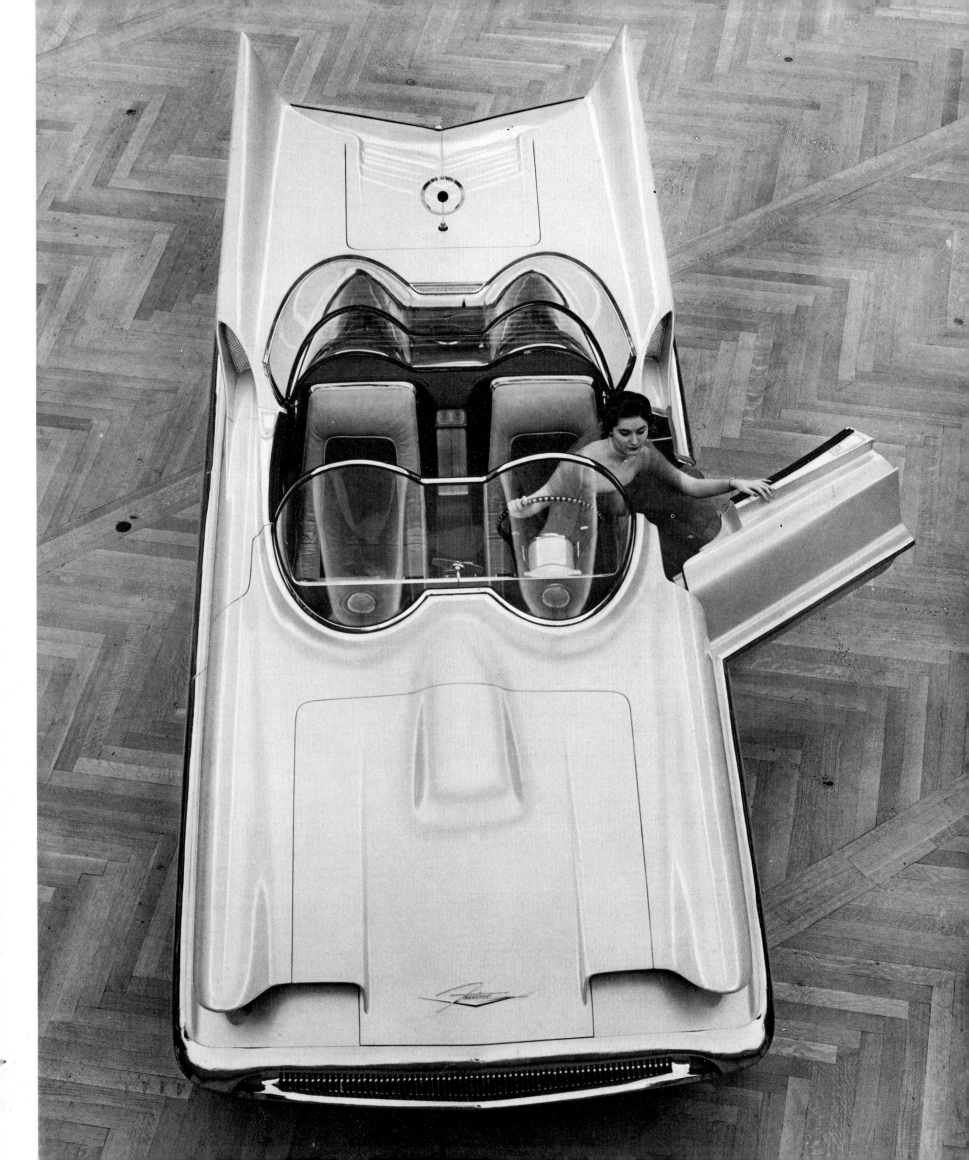

1954 — Buick Wildcat II The Wildcat II, like the experimental convertible of the same name introduced by Buick the previous year, had a fibreglass body. Although Chevrolet later made use of this material for the body of the Corvette, it was never used in any of Buick's production models. They never made a production model as small (14 ft 4 ins long and 3 ft 11 ins to the top of the windscreen) or as light in weight either. Originally the car carried a stylised wild cat bonnet mascot and headlamps mounted on either side of the windscreen. These were later moved, no doubt because of legal considerations, to a position where they also helped to mask less attractive aspects of the exposed suspension elements. True to contemporary tastes, the interior was a combination of leather, aluminium, and chrome.

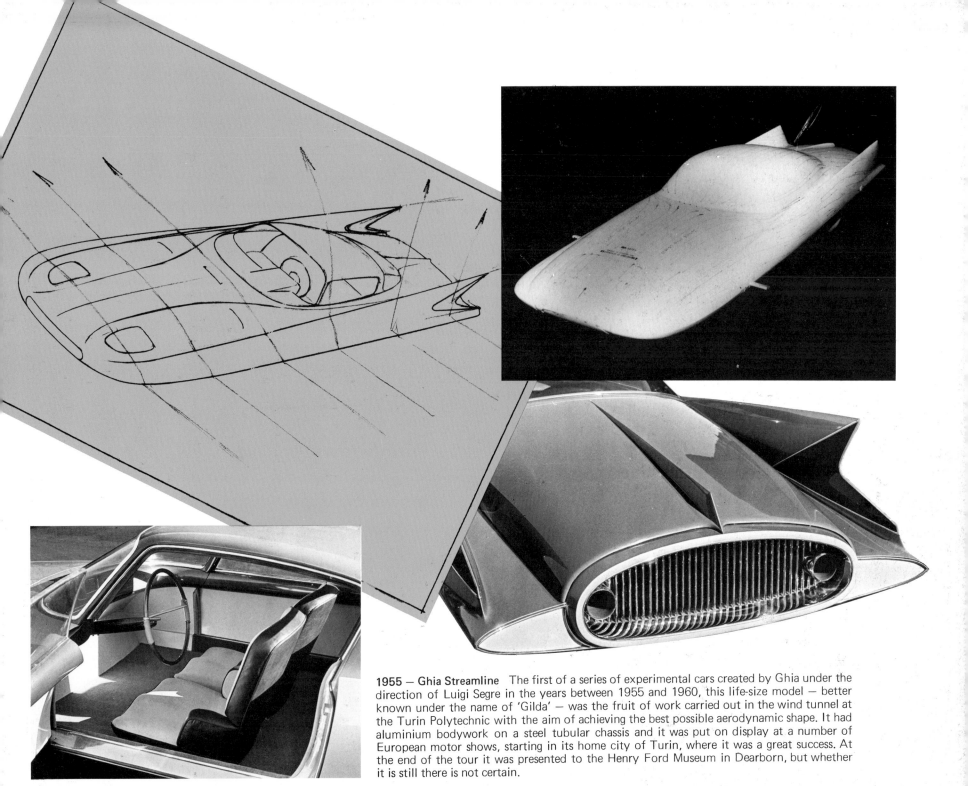

1955 — Ghia Streamline The first of a series of experimental cars created by Ghia under the direction of Luigi Segre in the years between 1955 and 1960, this life-size model — better known under the name of 'Gilda' — was the fruit of work carried out in the wind tunnel at the Turin Polytechnic with the aim of achieving the best possible aerodynamic shape. It had aluminium bodywork on a steel tubular chassis and it was put on display at a number of European motor shows, starting in its home city of Turin, where it was a great success. At the end of the tour it was presented to the Henry Ford Museum in Dearborn, but whether it is still there is not certain.

1954 — Oldsmobile Cutlass Two features of this high-performance — it had a 250 hp V8 engine — hardtop coupé were to re-appear again and again on dream cars and production models. They were the deeply cut-away front wheel arches, sometimes trimmed with chrome (or in this case stainless steel), which were popular on dream cars from GM in the 'sixties, and the rear window louvres, which are still in vogue today.

1954 — Pontiac Bonneville Special It was a visit to the famous land speed record site at the Bonneville salt flats in Utah which inspired Harley Earl to design this sports coupé powered by an in-line eight-cylinder engine fed through four carburetters. The similarity to the later Corvette is not surprising, since the Chevrolet sports car was also an Earl design.

The Chevrolet Corvette (in the foreground in the picture opposite) wrote a series of firsts in the automotive history books: amongst the dream cars, it was the first to go into series production; in the field of automobile production it was the world's first fibreglass production car; and in the development of the American automobile industry it was the first of a new breed of 'personal cars' which was to spawn the Thunderbird, Mustang and Camaro, among others. Yet its success came about mainly by chance. It was such a hit at the 1953 Motorama that it was immediately put into production. At first, only the first 300 production examples were to have been built in fibreglass — which was chosen as the material for the show car purely in order that it might be produced in the shortest possible time — and subsequent cars would have traditional steel bodies. In the event, public demand and improved production techniques led to the continuation of fibreglass construction. At the 1954 Motorama Chevrolet showed three Corvette derivatives — a hardtop with wind-down windows, a fast-back coupé, and a station wagon on a standard 1953 Chevrolet chassis, called the Nomad, the fore-runner of the production Bel Air Nomad model.

1954 — Cadillac El Camino A hardtop coupé which, according to its designers, featured 'aircraft styling' and 'supersonic' tailfins, the El Camino was named after the old Spanish road which became California's Highway 101. It had a brushed aluminium roof and a tinted windscreen, and horizontal flutes along the sides acted as camouflage for outlets for hot air from the engine compartment and intakes for cool air entering the passenger area.

1954 — Cadillac La Espada With a fibreglass body painted in 'Apollo Gold' and trimmed with chrome and aluminium, this twin sister of the Cadillac El Camino was an attractive vehicle. Notable aspects of the design were the extreme slope of the windshield and the way in which its pillar encroaches into the door opening, and the similarity in volume between the front and rear parts of the car. The convertible was 16 feet 8 inches long.

1955 — Rayon d'Azur A Lancia Aurelia GT 2500 chassis modified by Nardi with a body by Vignale. The double curvature windscreen is similar to that of the Ford Futura and the roof foreshadows what was to appear much later on the Corvette XP-700. The motif of a central metal air-intake in a plexiglass roof with sliding windows was also to re-appear, this time as a rear-view periscope, on the same Corvette and on the Corvette Shark. Even the colour treatment was similar, with two shades of blue being used on this car.

1955 — Chrysler Special Corsaire In 1953, Mario Boano left Ghia because he felt that the Chrysler influence was too strong. He founded his own coachbuilding company a year later and until 1957 he carried out work on both European and American chassis for such stylists as Exner and Loewy, as well as building his own creations. One of his first designs was this coupé with a Chrysler V8 engine in a Nardi-built tubular chassis, a buxom Italian with a strong American heart.

1955 — La Salle II The introduction of the La Salle marque in 1927 coincided with the recruitment of Harley Earl to General Motors, and it was his work on the first La Salle model for which he was responsible that earned him his place as head of Styling. The marque was dropped in 1940 but the name was revived in 1955 for two Cadillac show cars for the General Motors Motorama show of that year. A six-passenger saloon and a two-seater sports, the cars embodied both old and new styling influences in their grilles, with vertical ports based on the pre-war La Salle shape combined with modern 'bullet' bumper fairings. Similar echoes of the past are to be found in the rear wings with their deeply-recessed wheel-arches, and the front wings with their pronounced cut-away. On the other hand, the way in which the windscreen curved back into the roof was entirely new, as was the manner in which the exhausts were fed through the body sills to exit through titanium ports ahead of the rear wheels. Lighter, lower, and smaller than contemporary production models, the La Salle II's were powered by V6 engines equipped with fuel-injection and developing 150 hp. Aluminium wheels had the brake-drums cast integrally with them and the finned wheel design served not only as a styling accent, but also as a means of cooling the brakes. This feature was also used on the Pontiac Firebird I. The saloon was only 15 feet long and 4 feet 2 inches high — compact by American standards of 1955 — and was painted the same metallic blue as the Le Sabre with matching upholstery. The coupé was 12 feet 8 inches long.

The 1955 Motorama attracted 2,337,000 visitors who saw, amongst other attractions, the La Salle II saloon flanked by the Pontiac Strato-Star and the Buick Wildcat III.

1955 — Pontiac Strato-Star 'Concavities (sic) in the front fenders behind the wheels give the Strato-Star the sports car look'. That was the official GM line in 1955. From the same family of show cars as the La Salle II and the Chevrolet Biscayne, the Strato-Star was powered by the Strato-Streak V8 producing 250 hp in four carburetter form and had an interior trimmed in red with brushed aluminium highlights. There was seating capacity for six — so a 'sports car look' was as near to high performance as it was likely to get.

1956 — Cadillac Eldorado Brougham Town Car Everything about this car — even its name — was longer, or wider, or more luxurious than other cars. Nearly eighteen and a half feet long, it was six feet six inches wide and four feet seven inches high. Contained within these generous dimensions was everything the millionaire could wish for — a bar, a radio-telephone, a cigar humidor, air-conditioning, and a vanity unit for his lady. Interior trim was in black morocco leather in the front compartment and beige leather and cloth at the rear. The body was of fibreglass, and it had a central door-locking system.

1955 — Buick Wildcat III The last of Buick's series of savage felines, this open four-seater (also shown on page 49) did not achieve the success of the earlier Wildcat II, probably because its body was too closely based on one of the company's production cars and its grille, whilst unusual for a Buick, was very similar to that of Ford's Thunderbird.

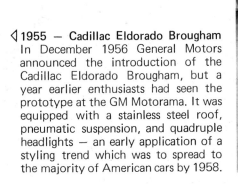

◁ 1955 — Cadillac Eldorado Brougham In December 1956 General Motors announced the introduction of the Cadillac Eldorado Brougham, but a year earlier enthusiasts had seen the prototype at the GM Motorama. It was equipped with a stainless steel roof, pneumatic suspension, and quadruple headlights — an early application of a styling trend which was to spread to the majority of American cars by 1958.

1955 — Oldsmobile 88 Delta This four-seat hardtop owed its individuality to its channelled waistline design and the way in which the oval forward part of the front wings housed the headlamps, driving lights and an air-intake for the front brakes. Aluminium was used for the wheels and the roof and the fibreglass body was finished in two shades of blue, with blue-tinted glass and a blue roof.

1954 — Pontiac Strato Streak According to its publicists, 'this exclusive show car incorporates many features which some day may be standard on the car of the future.' These included 'aerodynamic lines emphasised by wind-splits which start on the roof and carry down the rear deck', a 'panoramic' windscreen, a multiplicity of windows to give all-round vision, front seats which swivelled through 90 degrees for easy exit, and push-button controls hidden behind the steering-wheel. Pillarless construction had been a feature of 'cars of the future' since the 'thirties, as had pretty girls. The only trouble was that the doors, like the girls, sagged with age.

1954 — Oldsmobile F-88 There was more than a hint of the Corvette about this two-seater, particularly in the side view. Other elements of the design were unique, however; the transparent headlamp fairings and the stylised '88' covering a dummy air outlet on the front wings were two of them. A bonnet-top air-intake, honeycomb grille, and styled wheels all helped to give the convertible body a performance image and the Rocket engine's power output of 250 hp helped the car to live up to it.

1955 — Chevrolet Biscayne Which has dated more, the model's outfit or the car's styling ? The advantage of female fashion is that everything comes back into style sooner or later, but the same is not true of cars. Show cars, like haute couture, are the fashions which influence the styles of tomorrow but in the case of this car only the new V8 engine of 4.3 litres capacity and the name, which was used for Chevrolets from 1959, were passed on to production. Perhaps that was for the best, when one sees the 'Astro-dome' windscreen, the concave side-panels and the grin formed by the proximity of headlights and grille.

1956 — Chrysler Dart or Super Gilda A practical expression of the aerodynamic research carried out with the Ghia Gilda, the Dart had functional lines of impressive simplicity. The body's framework was welded directly to the Chrysler A-498 chassis and clad in light-alloy panels, giving excellent rigidity coupled with low lines and good passenger space. The engine was a K300 V8 giving 375 bhp. The steel-panelled roof slid back into the rear compartment and could be operated when the car was stationary or in motion. The car, which was claimed to have only one third of the drag of a normal model, was finished in metallic grey with black for the roof and lower panels. It still exists, under the name of 'Diablo', in the hands of a Pennsylvania collector. The new name brought with it lowered fins, a fabric top, a new interior, and a new bright red colour.

1953 — Ford X-100 An example of an experimental car which provided styling ideas for subsequent production cars. The 'torpedo' styling of the sides was to appear on the Fairlane 500 of 1959 and the 1960 Starliner; the circular rear-lamp shape was to become a feature of Fords for some years; and the rear-end treatment was a shadow of Thunderbirds to come.

1956 — Ford X-1000 This was a project that never got beyond the 3/8-scale model stage, so we shall never know what the reactions would have been of motorists who met a full-size example on the road — or possibly in the air. 'If', 'possibly', and 'might be' were favourite words in the vocabulary of the writers who described Ford's cars of the future, and this was no exception.

According to the press release, the X-1000 'could conceivably accommodate any of several new types of power plant either at the front or the rear'. It's nice to see they didn't know how it could work either.

1956 — Ferrari 410 Superamerica The design of this sports coupé on the Ferrari 410 Superamerica chassis, with its 5 litre 300 hp engine, was heavily influenced by Ghia's Gilda, but this time the coachbuilder produced a more decorative front end. The combination of the headlights, bumpers, grille, and wings was very harmonious and blended naturally with the low-set protective chrome band which encircled the car.

1956 — Alfa Romeo Super Flow I An experimental body by Pininfarina, full of unusual features. Notice how the shape of the front overhang is designed to hold the front wheels down at high speed whilst the rear fins aid directional stability. Even more unusual are the clear sections in the wings over the over-sized front wheels and the door design, with the lower half opening in the normal manner whilst the window is hinged at the roof and swings upward.

1956 — Ford Mystère The mystery about this car is what was intended to be its power-plant — although the multiple air-intakes and perforated panels hint at a rear-mounted turbine. It also featured two components which were favourites with dream car designers — a transparent vaulted roof which lifted when the doors were opened and a steering-wheel which could be swung in front of either seat for left or right hand drive.

1956 — Chrysler Norseman A year of design work by Chrysler and fifteen months of craftsmanship by Ghia disappeared in July 1956 when the liner 'Andrea Doria' sank off the coast of North Carolina with the Chrysler Norseman in its hold. It was a show car that was never shown and those responsible for its design — in particular Virgil M. Exner and Bill Brownlie — were never able to see the car for which they had conceived so many novel features. Among those features were a cantilever roof which dispensed with the traditional screen and side pillars, a rear window which slid up into the roof, a body of mainly aluminium panels, retractable head-lamps mounted in the wing extremities, seat backs which pivoted along a vertical axis to allow easy access to the rear, and lap-type seat-belts which retracted into housings in the transmission tunnel when not in use.

1956 — Buick Centurion Open the door, and the bucket seat moves backward automatically. Push on the back of the front seats, and they move forward mechanically to make entry and exit from the rear seats more easy. Slip into the metal, leather, and fibreglass cockpit and stretch out your legs — there is plenty of room because there is no steering column in the way; it passes down the centre of the car and the wheel is supported in front of the driver on a cantilever arm. Engage reverse gear with a glance at the TV screen which has replaced the rear-view mirror; its camera is mounted at the rear above a bomb-shaped housing which hides the stop and reversing lights behind translucent material which looks like chrome — until the lights come on. The same dissimulation applies to the rear lights. The body of your coupé is moulded in fibreglass, the grille and bonnet (hood) forming one complete unit, hinged at the front.

59

1956 — Oldsmobile Golden Rocket Again an example of the stylists' obsession with 'easy access'. In this case, opening the door activated a panel in the roof which lifted in order to enable the occupants to get into seats which, by lifting and turning towards the outside, almost got out to meet them. Another aid to entry was a steering wheel which split when two buttons were pressed, allowing the lower part to fold away from the driver. Apart from the fact that it was 16 feet 9 inches long and had a 275 hp V8 in a fiberglass body, it would have made an ideal invalid car.

1956 — Chevrolet Corvette SR2 A real all-purpose car. It raced at Daytona, Sebring, and Road America, it was a star of the automobile show circuit, and was the personal transport of its happy creator, Bill Mitchell.

1956 — Mercury XM-Turnpike Cruiser Designed to make the most of the new motor roads which were being built at the time, this car was designed to 'give American motorists the maximum driving pleasure, comfort, and safety as they travel the new turnpikes'. The large glass area was described as 'a salient feature to permit full enjoyment of the wide new vistas opened to turnpike travellers'. The car itself became a seasoned 'turnpike traveller' as it crossed the United States en route to the many shows at which it was displayed. A specially-built trailer unit made the car as much an exhibit on the road as it was at the shows.

1956 — Packard Predictor Designed by Richard Teague, Packard's styling chief, with the assistance of Dick McAdam, the Predictor body was built by Ghia of Turin in 90 days to meet a tight deadline which would enable the car to be shown at the Chicago Auto Show. It was greeted with approval from all sides when it was put on display but despite support from the public, dealers, and share-holders, it was not enough to save the Packard company from foundering along with Studebaker half-way through 1956. Size was in keeping with American tastes of the period, and the styling was restrained, but there were some very innovative touches such as slide-away panels in the roof, similar to the front of a roll-top desk, which rolled back when the door was opened to give easier access. Swivelling front seats were another aid to entry and the reverse-slope rear window was later used by Ford for production cars.

1954 — Fiat 8001 Six years of research lay behind this project and it all came to nothing. In 1948 Inginiere Dante Giacosa of Fiat was given the task of developing a gas turbine suitable for automobile use and the first runs on the test-bed took place in 1953, after a number of difficult technical problems had been overcome. The engine consisted of three combustion chambers and three turbine stages, only one of which was driven, the other two driving a two-stage centrifugal compressor. It developed 200 hp at 20,000 rpm. No heat exchanger was fitted and circulating oil was the cooling medium. After a year the engine was fitted in the car and tests were started at the Lingotto test track. The tests, which were inconclusive, lasted only a month and it was not long before the 8001 disappeared from the scene. With temperatures at the entry stage of the turbine reaching 800 degrees Centigrade, it seems likely that insurmountable cooling problems coupled with excessive fuel consumption led to the experiment being abandoned. The car itself was based on the tubular chassis of the Fiat V8 Sport and was clothed with a body to which wind-tunnel research had given particularly smooth lines (a drag coefficient of 0.14 had been measured on scale models). The rear position of the turbine meant that air to feed it had to be led through ducts which traversed the whole body length from the nose air-intake to the rear engine compartment.

1956 — Pontiac Club de Mer Claustrophobes, fresh-air fiends, sun-tan specialists, and couples on the verge of divorce would seem to be the ideal customers for this, the smallest of the General Motors dream cars, measuring only 3 feet 2 inches to the top of the windscreen and 15 feet in length. The body was aluminium, anodised pale blue rather than being painted, and the tiny rear fin did not create the misgivings which it might in these post-'Jaws' days. Powered by a V8 Strato-Streak engine developing 300 horsepower, the car had a rear-mounted gearbox and a De Dion rear axle. Headlamps and driving lamps were mounted in rotating housings and were invisible when not in use. The Club de Mer, which was shown alongside the Oldsmobile Golden Rocket, was one of the premier attractions of the 1956 GM Motorama.

1958 — Ford La Galaxie Aeronautical influences at work again in the interior styling of another car which left nothing but its name as a contribution to later production cars. The odd-shaped wheel had the transmission and turn-signal controls built in to it, but would have required a fair degree of manual dexterity to accomplish a swift U-turn. Switches on the left of the binnacle control such vital items as seats, headrests, doors, and the twin boot-lids. In addition to all the usual controls and instruments, there was a 'communications control and a screen for a proposed proximity warning apparatus'.

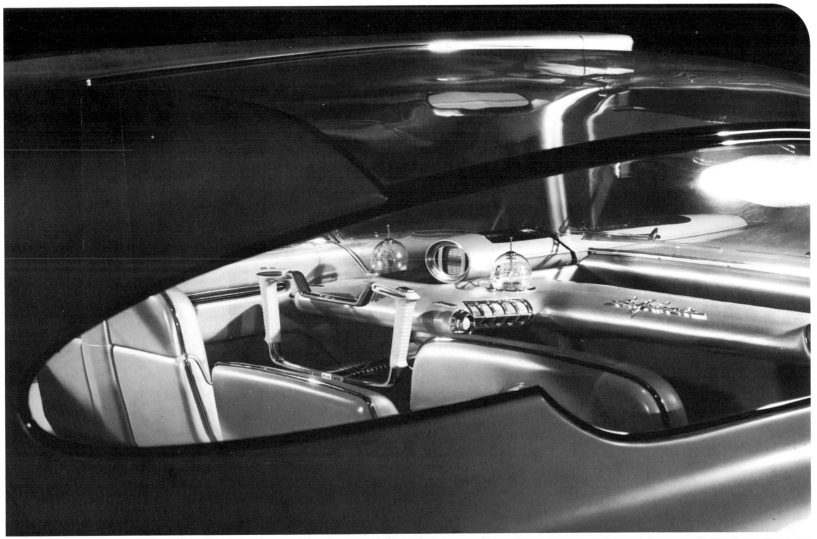

The exterior of the La Galaxie was at least different, and was pleasantly free of the excess of chrome of which so many stylists of the period were guilty. The rear end was dominated by the 'Vis-o-Rama' tail-lights and at the front was more evidence of the Ford stylists' ability to come up with styling for technological break-throughs which the engineers had unfortunately not yet made. This time it was 'two high-intensity fog-piercing lamps'.

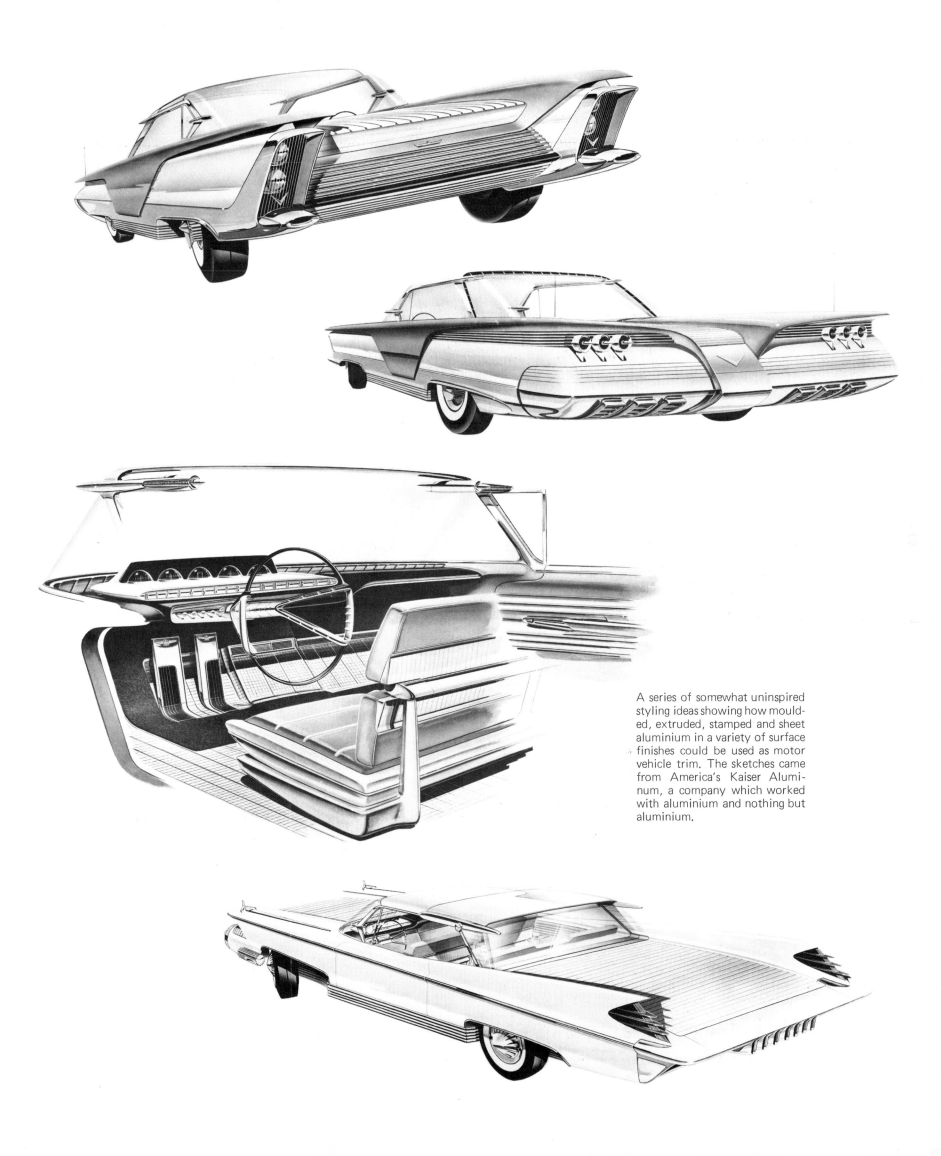

A series of somewhat uninspired styling ideas showing how moulded, extruded, stamped and sheet aluminium in a variety of surface finishes could be used as motor vehicle trim. The sketches came from America's Kaiser Aluminum, a company which worked with aluminium and nothing but aluminium.

1957 — BMW Raymond Loewy The chassis was a German BMW 507 unit, the stylist was an American from New York who had distinguished himself in the world of automobile design with his work for Studebaker, and the body was built in France by the firm of Bernard Pichon and André Parat. This international combination produced the car which Raymond Loewy showed at the Paris Show in 1957 and which created a great deal of interest because of its unusual lines. The doors cut into the roof and the rear window was in smoked plexiglass, the exhausts exited through the rear over-riders, and the BMW badge was likened to a gun sight by which the driver could aim the car.

1957 — Chevrolet Corvette SS One of the cherished babies of Zora Arkus-Duntov, Corvette tuner extraordinaire. This one had a multi-tubular chassis, magnesium-alloy body panels in a style reminiscent of the Jaguar D Type, and a 4.6 litre V8 producing 315 hp. The car was entered for the Sebring sports car race of 1957 but retired after 35 laps. A plan to run in it in the Le Mans 24-Hour race was thwarted by a ruling from the Automobile Manufacturers Association in America which, frightened by the escalation in horse-power, forbade their members to go racing.

1958 — Imperial D'Elegance One can forgive this lapse by Virgil M. Exner in view of the quality of his previous creations. Unfortunately it was to influence certain aspects of Chrysler's later production models.

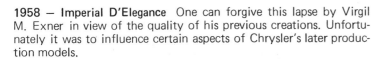

1958 — Simca Fulgur Another view of the future expressed as a full-size (non-working) model. The Fulgur was to have been powered by two rear-mounted electric motors and the driver, acting on information received from his radar sets, would transmit his orders to the car through the medium of an electronic brain which would take charge of actually driving the vehicle. On the motorway the Fulgur would be controlled — at no extra charge — by a central control tower. Running under an automatic pilot, it would draw power for the motor by means of induction. Over 150 km per hour the front wheels would retract. And so on and so on...

1958 — Ford Nucleon A 3/8-scale model ▷ of what Ford's stylists thought an atomic-powered car would look like, assuming that it would be possible to reduce the size and weight of the necessary reactors. It was their feeling that the power-plant would be mounted in a protective capsule between the rear fins and that there would be a range of interchangeable units with different power outputs.

1958 — Ford X-2000 'Although it is ▷ highly unlikely that this particular model will ever become a production vehicle, it is possible that some of its features may be adapted for use in future production cars' said Ford's hand-out at the time. Don't hold your breath waiting for them.

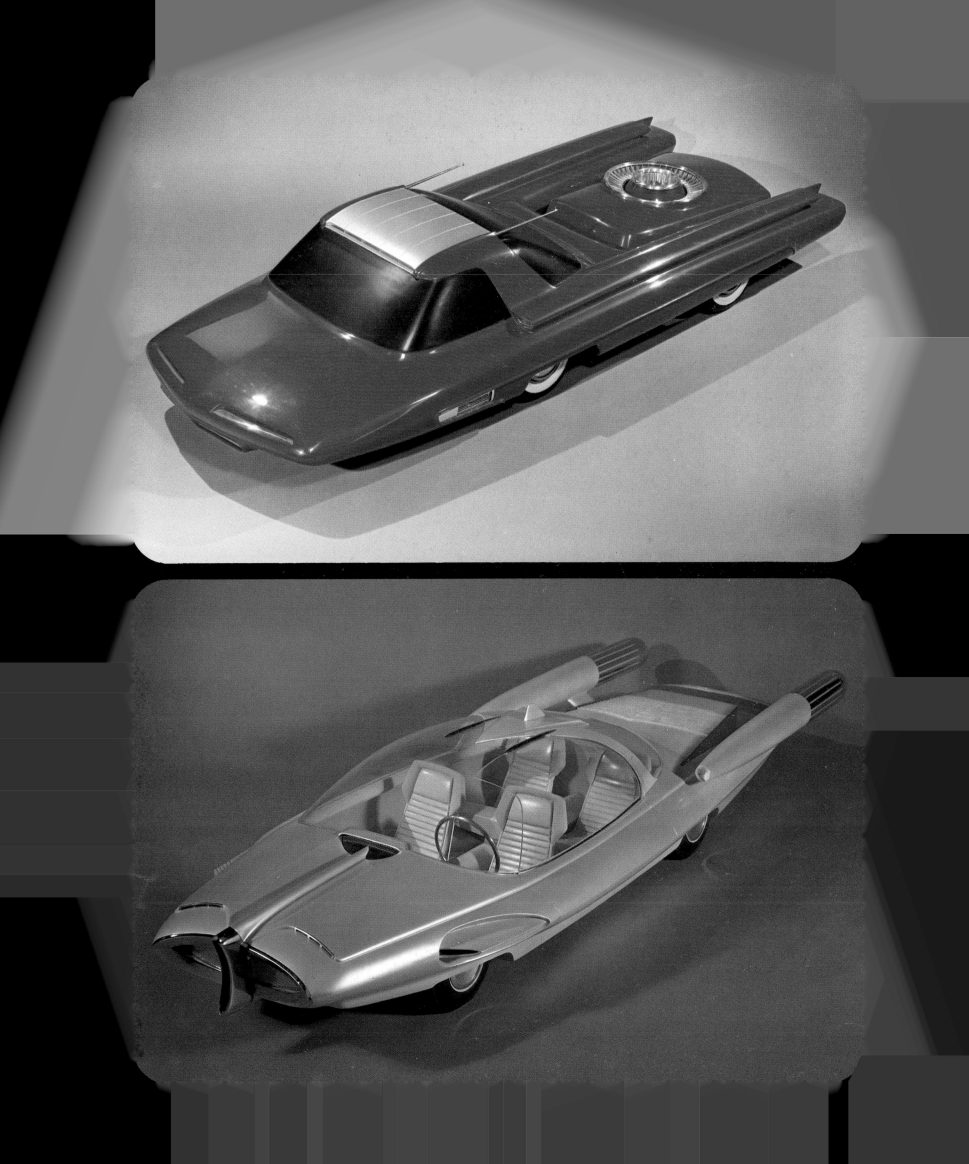

1954 — XP-21 Firebird This single-seater experimental vehicle was America's first turbine car, built round a 370 hp unit by General Motors' research laboratories at Warren and fitted with a fibreglass body constructed under the direction of Harley Earl. The car had a gearbox giving two forward speeds and reverse, a de Dion rear axle, and a braking system which allied air-brakes in the 'fuselage' to finned drum brakes mounted outside the wheel bearings for cooling and accessibility.

1956 — Firebird II Although the second Firebird was also an experimental vehicle, it was designed as a family car and had four seats. In addition to being suitable for use on normal roads, it was also equipped with the necessary elements to make it capable of operating on a remote-controlled highway system which GM has suggested at their 1956 Motorama. The power plant was an improved 200 hp unit developed by the GM research laboratories. It was equipped with a heat-exchanger which recuperated four-fifths of the exhaust heat to heat the incoming air. For the first time, titanium was used in an automobile body and the vehicle had an electro-magnetically controlled 4-speed gearbox. Self-levelling hydro-pneumatic suspension gave a smooth ride and information was passed to the driver by means of two TV screens, one of which replaced the rear-view mirror. The other served as part of the remote-control guidance system and displayed maps and other information to be beamed out by a central control tower and received by the two aerials mounted in the air-intake cones. The heavily aircraft-influenced front end is notable for the unusual treatment of the retractable headlamps.

74

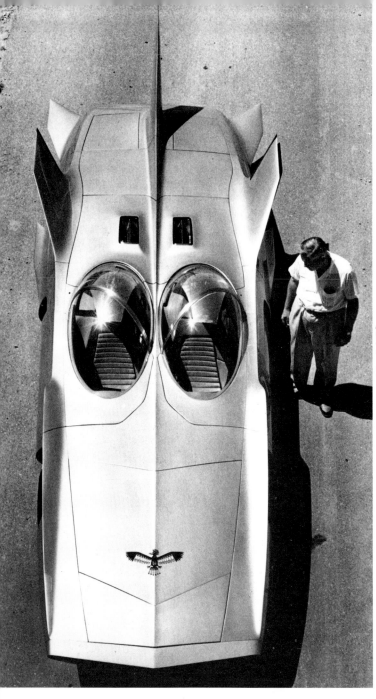

1958 — Firebird III Under a body which was designed to look like 'a vehicle you might ride in to the astroport for a trip to the moon', as Harley Earl put it, were so many technical innovations that there is only space to list a selection : a single central control lever, accessible from both seats, which controlled steering, acceleration, and braking; a speed-hold device — now better-known as 'cruise-control'; automatic control systems developed from those in Firebird II; remote door-opening by means of ultrasonic control; air-conditioning which maintained the car's interior at a constant temperature even when it was standing still; automatic illumination of the lamps; a power unit which although more powerful (225 hp) was also 25 per cent more economical; electroluminescent instrument displays; and an anti-skid braking system which gave optimum stopping-power whatever the road conditions.

1957 — Cadillac Brougham A year before, this interior trim — with its seats like Second Empire sofas, sheepskin rugs and profusion of chrome — had been a feature of a GM dream car. Now it appeared in this limited-edition Cadillac and the thousand examples which were built were described as the most luxurious and technically complex cars ever offered to the American public.

1958 — Buick Wells Fargo A production car modified to show car standards according to the wishes of Dale Robertson, the star of the 'Wells Fargo' TV series. He would obviously feel at home in a car whose seats were trimmed in leather decorated with embossed patterns and pokerwork designs based on those of western saddles. The twin Winchesters between the front seats might be just a little too tempting for today's frustrating driving conditions, however.

1961 — Buick Flamingo Another example of a production Buick with a custom interior. This one would obviously appeal to those passengers who prefer not to see what the driver is doing — or maybe it is just a follow-up to the Wells Fargo car and gives the man riding shotgun a better view of the pursuing Cherokees ?

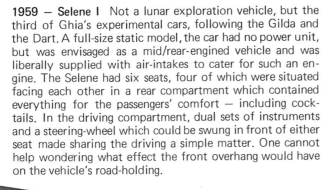

1959 — Selene I Not a lunar exploration vehicle, but the third of Ghia's experimental cars, following the Gilda and the Dart. A full-size static model, the car had no power unit, but was envisaged as a mid/rear-engined vehicle and was liberally supplied with air-intakes to cater for such an engine. The Selene had six seats, four of which were situated facing each other in a rear compartment which contained everything for the passengers' comfort — including cocktails. In the driving compartment, dual sets of instruments and a steering-wheel which could be swung in front of either seat made sharing the driving a simple matter. One cannot help wondering what effect the front overhang would have on the vehicle's road-holding.

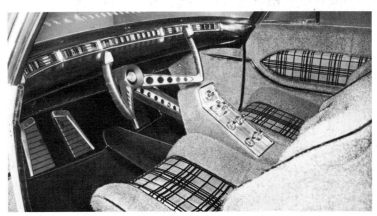

1959 — Scimitar Based on a Chrysler chassis, this aluminium body was designed by the American stylist Brooks Stevens and built by Reutter of Stuttgart. Equipped with a mechanically retractable metal hard-top, it was more interesting than beautiful.

1959 — Cadillac Starlight The line is uncluttered and slender and there is an absence of unnecessary chrome. The light and airy plexiglass roof has four metal panels which slide into place to protect the occupants from the sun. The sure touch of Pininfarina is all over this experimental prototype.

1959 — Buick XP-75 The maximum exterior surface for the minimum interior space in this two-seater sports coupé based on the Buick Skylark. The fins, which up to now had been vertical appendages, are beginning to show a movement towards the horizontal position which they were to reach in the early 'sixties.

1959 — De Soto Cella I A 3/8-scale model of a car to be driven by a fuel cell — which was a spin-off from space technology and produced electrical energy from the interaction of hydrogen and oxygen. The current was to be used to drive separate motors at each of the wheels. Advantage of the system would have been silence, and simplicity of operation and maintenance. The lack of transmission components meant a low and completely flat floor-pan. The Cella I would have been equipped with a number of electronic devices to control the relative speeds of the four motors and thus to avoid wheel-spin and skids. Once again the designers replaced one of the simplest components in a car — the rear-view mirror — with something more complicated, this time a wide-angle periscope system.

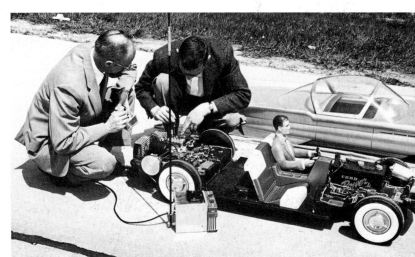

1959 — Ford La Tosca Ford addressed themselves to the stylist's problem of assessing how a design would look when it was in motion by building this 3/8-scale radio-controlled chassis to carry mock-ups of future styling projects.

1959 — Cadillac Cyclone Having exhausted the inspirational effect of aircraft, the American stylists turned their attentions towards space. In its modified 1960 version, with re-styled fins, wheels and rear-end, the Cyclone had the abstract beauty of a missile. The 'nose-cones' on the forward part of the wings housed radar sets which provided the driver with visual and audible warning of obstacles in his path, the intensity of the signals increasing as the object came closer. The retractable top lifted automatically when the doors — which slid back longitudinally along the sides of the car — were opened. The Cyclone featured an intercom for passengers to talk to those outside the car and an automatic cruise control — both of which had first appeared on the Firebird III.

1960 — Plymouth XNR The XNR owed its name to its designer, Virgil M. Exner, Chrysler's styling chief. In this very personal expression of his design philosophy, Exner said he was 'striving to avoid the static and bulky, which is ugly and not what an automobile should look like. The goal is to try for the graceful look, with a built-in feeling of motion. The wedge shape expresses the function of automobiles because it imparts a sense of direction'. Construction of the XNR was entrusted to Ghia.

◁ **1958 — Chevrolet Corvette XP700** Originally built as the personal car of William L. Mitchell, this car incorporated ideas which he wanted to use in future Corvette and other GM cars and was the first of a series of experimental cars produced under his direction. Unlike many of the static Motorama display cars, these were fully operational. The XP700 was built on a 1958 Corvette convertible chassis and its front-end treatment inspired the Oldsmobile F88, whilst its rear was used for the 1961 model Corvette. The XP700 was converted into a 'Show Car' in 1959 by the addition of a transparent top, a periscope, an oval grille in a larger oval air-intake, and an elongated rear deck. It is shown in this form opposite.

1961 — Chrysler Turboflite Chrysler's first turbine car, designed by company stylists and built by Ghia. The top was raised and lowered automatically by opening and closing the doors — and could be used to decapitate unwelcome passengers if necessary. The side windows were hinged in the roof and the rear wing rotated to act as an air-brake.

The Golden Age of dream cars

SERGIO PININFARINA The 'fifties were a time of optimism; the war had just finished and there was a climate of expansion in all sectors of the economy. Our society was expanding, full of creative activity and new ideas, and for Europeans in general and Italians in particular the automobile represented a new field of success. It is only normal that such a period of expansion should have found its expression in the field of the automobile industry with its potential for exploring so many new areas of technology and style.

FILIPPO SAPINO – GHIA The greater part of the dream cars built during the golden age of the dream car—that is the late 'fifties and early 'sixties—seem to have been designed on the premise that some day all cars would have wings and would fly. It was certainly a happier era, free of the problems which affect the car industry today. The dream cars were probably an expression of optimism, of confidence in the future, but mainly they grew from a stronger love of the car, which in those days was not seen as the source of problems which it is today.

GIORGIO GIUGIARO – ITAL DESIGN The dream car belongs to a certain period of automotive history and is closely linked with the coach builder's profession. Before, the coachbuilder manufactured small numbers of very special vehicles and needed 'special' ideas to fulfill the needs of his production facilities. Today, they have extended their means of production and have chosen to become advisers to the big manufacturers. On the one hand the prototypes were for small production numbers, and on the other they are for series production.

R.F. ZOKAS – FORD At that time labour and material costs were far less than today and companies had more money to spend on such things. In addition, it was the postwar era and the public was hungry for anything new in automobiles.

IRVIN W. RYBICKI – GENERAL MOTORS It was an era when the public was extremely interested in such cars and we had many ideas we wanted to express and 'show off'.

NUCCIO BERTONE The construction of a prototype involves around 15,000 hours of work, often 'stolen' from the normal work of the establishment. There was a time when nearly all those hours were overtime work. The rigidity of work contracts and agreements today is a simple explanation of why it was easier to build prototypes in the 'fifties and 'sixties.

PAUL BRACQ The dream cars were the symbol of the American economic explosion in the 'fifties, as the Italian prototypes were a symbol of the rennaissance of industry and the sports car in that country.

WILLIAM M. BROWNLIE – CHRYSLER CORPORATION After the Second World War the art of car styling – design, as it is now known – was just getting into its stride and all the major companies formed their own 'styling departments'. The explosion of ideas which this gave rise to resulted in a series of dream cars which were seen as an excellent way to test public reaction to these new ideas. There was a tremendous amount of energy at that time and a tremendous amount of pressure from the companies to advance the design of the automobile. This of course led to the heads of the various styling departments pushing their design staffs to be more creative. Coupled with this was the fact that the corporations were willing to spend money to turn dream cars into reality, and this meant that the whole thing flourished.

85

Dream cars in relation to the future

NUCCIO BERTONE   As far as I personally am concerned, I have to say that a large number of the cars which we have shown as prototypes have become production models in the course of time, either as complete vehicles or as the basis of developed versions. The complete list is too long to give here, but I would say the best-known examples of our prototypes—and their production counterparts—are Miura (Lamborghini Miura), Montreal (Alfa Romeo Montreal), Runabout (Fiat X 1/9), Stratos (Lancia Stratos), and Countach (Lamborghini Countach). I think that gives a very good idea of how often a prototype can be the origin of a production model—and that's not considering the points of detail design which are later used in production models.

FILIPPO SAPINO — GHIA   The visions and hopes which I spoke about with reference to the golden days of the dream cars were, as we can now see, to be disappointed. The way in which our times have fallen short of the optimism and confidence which those cars of twenty years ago showed is something which should sadden all of us.

R.F. ZOKAS — FORD   Nobody can predict the future accurately. There are too many continual changes to our economy, society and environment for a designer to design a car exactly correct for the period he was originally aiming for.

PAUL BRACQ   The 'dreams' of the stylists of the past were limited by the technology of their times. The chassis and mechanical elements were derived directly from classic concepts and there was a total lack of integration between the styling and mechanical elements when it came to producing a 'view of the future'.

IRVIN W. RYBICKI — GENERAL MOTORS   The idea of hanging a specific date onto a dream car comes from the press, not us. When we showed a dream car at one of our Motoramas it was always just that—an expression of a dream as we saw it at the time we designed it.

SERGIO PININFARINA   On the contrary; I believe that these 'dream cars' which appear to be an end in themselves, have been in a great many cases the means to find solutions and express concepts which have proved valuable for a long time afterwards. I'm speaking of dream cars which are the result of real research into technical and styling concepts, of course, and not the kind of extravagant creations built purely as a 'crowd-pleaser'.

GIORGIO GIUGIARO — ITAL DESIGN   I do not agree. Hundreds of ideas which were tried on dream cars by the great coachbuilders have found their way into production models. No dream car has ever been produced in quantity, it is true, but how many times do dreams come true? As to foretelling the future, I often tell journalists who ask me what the car of the 'nineties will look like, that it will be in keeping with the styles in houses, clothes, hair, etc. of the time.

WILLIAM M. BROWNLIE — CHRYSLER CORPORATION   That is a very difficult question. We always have a certain period in mind when we create these cars for the future, and sometimes the prediction is right. On other occasions there may have been changes in economic conditions or public tastes which mean that we miss our guess. In the final analysis, however, even though we may not have got the mood of the times right, I think that it is all valid material.

The decline of the dream car

FILIPPO SAPINO – GHIA I think that the real dream car is dead. We are building a more restricted number of 'show cars' than we used to because of the cost and the fact that it is much more difficult to create a car which is as realistic and functional as possible while complying with regulations which are more and more restrictive.

SERGIO PININFARINA The problems today are very different from those of the 'fifties and 'sixties. In view of the present high level of costs, there is a preference for work which is more directly based on true scientific research. I do not consider the problems posed by today's regulations as insurmountable, nor are they purely negative influences. In fact there were certain limitations which applied to the early cars and which were simply due to the mechanical structure of the motor vehicle. Although these limitations existed, they did not constitute real obstacles to the stylists of the day because they did not approach them with a negative point of view. A positive approach to today's regulations can be constructive, and I would cite as an example the case of modern integrated bumpers, which have led to some forms of 'soft' moulded noses and tails which are aesthetically very pleasing.

GIORGIO GIUGIARO – ITAL DESIGN The conditions of the time stimulate talent and give birth to creative and artistic activity. That has always been the case in every field of creativity. After wood, architects worked with stone, then with bricks, then with concrete, then with metal, then with… well, who knows what will be next? New materials, new technologies, safety requirements, aerodynamic considerations, the exhaustion of the world's resources of materials are not only constraints, but are also stimulants to the planner. Naturally the differences between one product and another are going to be pared down, and there is going to be a need for more and more research into both overall conception and details, but the qualities which determine the success or failure of a car will always remain.

R.F. ZOKAS – FORD I think that it is a sign of the times. High fabrication costs, federal regulations requiring large sums of money to be poured into new programmes to meet those laws rather than dream cars. The public has also become a more sophisticated audience.

IRVIN W. RYBICKI – GENERAL MOTORS The present effort is on the improvement of the production car and the improvement today is going in very different directions from those it took in the past. Today we are concerned with serious issues such as occupant safety, aerodynamics, and energy efficiency. We are involved in extensive studies of vehicle aerodynamics and weight reduction. Developing solutions to these challenges takes serious research and development and a continuing design effort, the results of which will be seen in better products in the future. The growing regulations are a part of our design challenge just as are all the other facts that surround us today which are different from what they were a few years ago. We look at these changes in our environment as challenges to our design skills! We think that the future is bright and there is an ever-increasing public appreciation of good design. The need for fresh imaginative solutions is greater than ever. No amount of government regulations will ever cause new lines on paper. The new lines on the paper will come from the creative imagination of our best people. We see a resurgence of interest in good design. There is a growth in enrollment in design schools and a broad public demand for good new design. We see a bright future ahead for personal transportation and expect to be leading contributors to its development.

WILLIAM M. BROWNLIE — CHRYSLER CORPORATION I think that there are many factors which decide whether we are going to build dream cars or not, and basically it boils down to economics. There is no question that regulation has imposed an awful lot of pressure, and it has taken an awful lot of time, money, and energy to develop it properly. To some degree perhaps regulation has had a slight effect on the number of dream cars, but I think that the financial reasons are more important. Dream cars have rocketed in cost over the last few years and I feel that is why you see fewer and fewer of them.

NUCCIO BERTONE The network of international regulations, ever more constricting, limits the operating area of the stylist more and more. This is particularly true of production cars, but less so for prototypes, which are often now closer to what could be called, in scientific terms, pure research vehicles. These, by their nature, are limited by the considerations inherent in the research function.

R.F. ZOKAS — FORD Motor cars will always be a function of the imagination both to the designer and the public, but higher costs and regulations have had a dampening effect on dream cars as we knew them in the past.

PAUL BRACQ It is certain that the regulations are becoming more and more constricting, but it is up to the designers to make stronger and more daring explorations into their imaginations. The imagination and innovative capacity of a good designer knows no bounds.

The costs of a dream car

In examining the costs given—here in dollars at the then rate of exchange—it will be noticed that there are not many: manufacturers and coachbuilders only quoted them (mostly in press communiqués or in subsequent interviews) when they were thought sufficiently low to justify continuing the experiments or high enough to demonstrate the large amount of effort put in. It will also be noted that it is difficult to compare them: some represent the expenses of a vast research programme, the building of entirely new engines, chassis and bodywork (Buick Le Sabre); others the costs for body and accessories clothing a model using chassis etc. taken from current production (Plymouth XX 500). Cost prices for prototypes built in Italy are lower than American-built dream cars for obvious reasons—cheaper labour, smaller firms, projects realised much more quickly.

1950	Buick Le Sabre—General Motors	500,000 dollars
1951	Plymouth XX 500 built by Ghia	10,000 dollars
1951	Chrysler K-310 built by Ghia	20,000 dollars
1953	Chevrolet Corvette—General Motors	55,000 dollars
1955	Lincoln Futura—Ford. Built by Ghia	250,000 dollars
1956	Packard Predicator	70,000 dollars
1961	Dodge Flitewing built by Ghia	125,000 dollars
1963	Corvair Testudo—Bertone. Put on sale by the coachbuilder in 1974 at a price of:	10,000 dollars
1965-69	Chevrolet Corvette Mako Shark II, later Manta Ray—General Motors	2,500,000 dollars
1976	Ferrari Rainbow—Bertone. Offered by Marshall Field in 1979 at a price of:	200,000 dollars
1977	Ford Megastar I built by Ghia	150,000 dollars
1978	Il Tempo Gigante by Ivo Caprino	150,000 dollars

Replicars—the dream cars of today?

NUCCIO BERTONE   There is a great feeling of nostalgia in art and the cinema, as well as in female fashions, so it is possible that the influence is also being felt in the world of the automobile. However, like all fashions, it is only a passing phase.

SERGIO PININFARINA   These replicas draw their inspiration from a period particularly good for car design, which had reached a maturity and style it had previously lacked. Some of the convertibles and sports cars of the 'thirties were truly classic designs, and I am not surprised that in the general rebirth of styles from that period, automobile styling has also looked back a little. However, it only concerns a few specialised vehicles and it is not really a trend which affects the industry in general.

IRVIN W. RYBICKI — GENERAL MOTORS   Replicars are a kind of nostalgia which has little to do with the future. They may have a limited market for some time. I think they are a strictly temporary fad.

FILIPPO SAPINO — GHIA   The success of the replica cars can be regarded as a reaction against the apparent impossibility of escaping from the iron restrictions which surround the modern automobile. In the field of cars, as in others, when one looks at the future and the view of ever-increasing pragmatism which it affords, the only escape possible seems to be towards a past which seems more pleasant than the present, mainly because it is seen in the light of memories of a special kind.

GIORGIO GIUGIARO — ITAL DESIGN   This recollection of the cars of another epoch is a cultural phenomenon. The automobile has entered into the history of human activity in the same way as have coins, stamps, furniture, and porcelain. To appreciate and collect the artifacts of the past is a human instinct going back to the beginnings of civilisation and I think that replicars are not just a passing fad, but represent an activity which will grow in importance and which will see constructors turning out limited production runs of old vehicles.

PAUL BRACQ   Replicars and 'period cars' are limited-production cars which are easier to produce than dream cars. They call for little creativity on the part of their builders because they are just copies of old cars, more or less adapted to modern mechanical parts. I think that this nostalgic trend is evidence of a time when people are afraid of the future; in fact, it is in just such periods that the activity of 'dreaming' should be exercised to the full in order to give confidence in the future.

WILLIAM M. BROWNLIE — CHRYSLER CORPORATION   I think it is basically due to nostalgia. There have been some great periods of automobile design, particularly the 'thirties with such makes as the Duesenberg, and I feel that there is a great urge to re-create that kind of car and capture some of the nostalgia. In addition, there is the question of the way modern design has been forced by federalisation and regulation to a point where, although the industry does its best, the cars are all beginning to look alike. Faced with this, some customers will buy replicars to have a little individuality. I think that some of the replicar builders are doing a really good job in terms of quality of manufacture, but the market is very small and I don't see replicars selling more than a few hundred cars a year—even if they would like to sell more.

American dream cars are limousines, Italian are sports cars—why?

IRVIN W. RYBICKI — GENERAL MOTORS No, it is not true. The dream cars were almost all much smaller, lighter, and more fun than the production cars of their day. America's No. 1 sports car, the Corvette, began its life as a show car in the Motorama of 1953! The dimensions of the La Salle dream car of 1955 were almost exactly those of the new models of 1979.

GIORGIO GIUGIARO — ITAL DESIGN As a general rule, it is true, probably because the limousine fits into the American scene and would correspond to the dreams of motorists in that country. An inhabitant of Florence would not dream of owning a Cadillac in that city—and if he did, the dream would soon become a nightmare.

FILIPPO SAPINO — GHIA It is not possible to generalise like that. Turin has turned out some fine saloon designs whilst there have been sporting coupés from Detroit.

SERGIO PININFARINA Europe—and particularly Italy—has a very strong sports car tradition compared to the U.S. and I need only mention the examples of Alfa Romeo, Ferrari, and Maserati to support this statement. It is only normal that such a rich potential would suggest styling ideas of an essentially sporting character.

NUCCIO BERTONE It is not my place to explain why Detroit prefers to build limousines, but I do know why we prefer to exhibit sports prototypes at motor shows. Parallel to our activity as stylists, in which we design and build normal production saloons for a number of clients, we have our own production facilities, capable of producing more than a hundred cars a day. This activity is kept going by small and medium-sized production runs. The production requirement for a saloon is beyond our capabilities in the majority of cases whereas the demand for sports models puts them well within our production capacity. This accounts for our preference for developing sporting cars for shows; they can provide the basis for work in our own production facilities.

R.F. ZOKAS — FORD I do not agree with this statement. Perhaps this impression exists due to the many replicars that are built today; after all, they are slightly modified vehicles on existing Detroit chassis. Ghia has created many small sports car-type dream cars for Europe and the U.S.

PAUL BRACQ The American market has always been orientated towards the large saloon car—the Corvette has been the only American sports car for what will soon be twenty-five years. The Italian sports car constructors have always provided magnificent chassis to the master coachbuilders of Turin and the marvellous creations they have built on them have served as excellent advertisements for the Italian automobile industry.

WILLIAM M. BROWNLIE — CHRYSLER CORPORATION I think that it is a result of the driving habits and culture of people in each of the countries. European cars have always been small, and I think that the people there were always excited by small, two-seater sports cars, so all the great sports cars seem to have come out of Turin. In the U.S., on the other hand, we were more affluent, we had a road system that meant you could drive 3000 miles coast-to-coast non-stop and that led to big automobiles.

Why are Japanese dream cars so rare?

SERGIO PININFARINA The first contacts between the western world and Japan took place only just over a century ago. Up to that time the country led an almost medieval way of life, but since then it has set out to catch up with the west and has become one of the most important of the world's industrial powers, with extremely competitive products of all kinds. However, in the world of the automobile, it probably lacks the specific cultural background of the western countries, and I think that this is the explanation for the fact that the car is regarded in Japan as a commercial, rather than creative entity.

NUCCIO BERTONE In my opinion, the Japanese excel in the organisation of their work and are perfect businessmen who would rather play it safe, without risking or compromising their plans. No other business operation in the world would display the prototypes of its new models without having first patented the new ideas it was showing and without having made detailed plans for the rapid commercialisation of those ideas and plans. It may be that only we, the Europeans, are prepared to let everyone have the benefit of our inspiration and ideas. To think that we have made a present of the ideas contained in about thirty prototypes in fifteen years! I wonder if we are sufficiently creative—or crazy—to hope to stay at the top for ever?

IRVIN W. RYBICKI — GENERAL MOTORS The facts are that as the Japanese have grown in importance in world trade, they have also become more courageous in experimental and dream car design. The most recent Tokyo Automobile Shows had several experimental cars on display and their

magazines also show increasing interest in exploratory work of all kinds. As world trade continues to expand, we expect increasing competition in all aspects of automobile design from all countries.

R.F. ZOKAS — FORD I have no idea.

FILIPPO SAPINO — GHIA I think that the Japanese have a number of difficulties in producing dream cars, but I am convinced that they like them enormously and would very much like to be able to produce them.

GIORGIO GIUGIARO — ITAL DESIGN It is a question of cultural background. The Japanese always think on an industrial scale. For them a single example of a commodity is a work of art, not a product, and belongs in a different aesthetic category. For them the automobile is a mass-produced product.

PAUL BRACQ The Japanese design studios now include some very gifted designers and I would not be surprised to see them give birth to a plethora of dream cars in a few years' time.

WILLIAM M. BROWNLIE — CHRYSLER CORPORATION I don't think that Japanese dream cars *are* rare. It is evident from the Tokyo Auto Shows that there has been a terrific growth in the interest in automobiles and I have found from my own visits to Japan that they are as car-conscious and as enthusiastic about dream cars as any other country in the world. I think that the Dome is an expression of their interest and their design approach to a dream car, showing, contrary to your question, that there is great activity.

91

1960-1961 — PFX and PFY These two Pininfarina experimental cars were the result of research into egg-shaped aerodynamic forms. On the X the shape was achieved by the unusual wheel configuration, but the Y was based on a standard four-seat production saloon with a conventional chassis.

1961 — Dodge Flitewing A new solution to the problem of entry posed by a four-seat coupé : when the front doors are opened, the windows, which are separate and hinged at roof-level, open like miniature gull-wing doors. When the doors are closed the windows swing down again — but a pressure-sensitive switch prevents them closing on a carelessly-positioned hand !

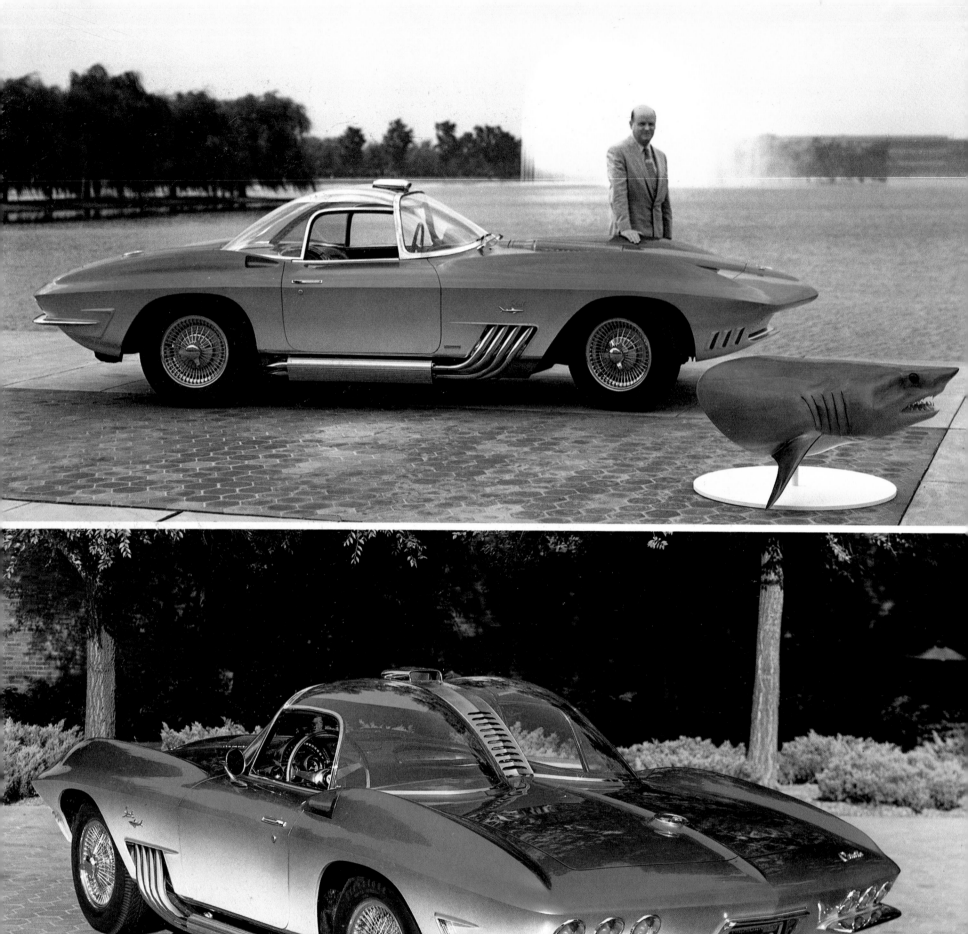

1960 — Selene Seconda Ghia presented the direct descendant of the Selene I as 'All ready for the 1970 Motor Show'. The new car had three seats and a rear-mounted engine. The driver was seated in the nose, ahead of the axle, and his two passengers were anti-socially placed with their backs to him. As a change from watching where they had been, they had a television set for their entertainment.

◁ **1962 — Chevrolet Corvette XP-755 Shark** When he designed this show car for the New York Auto Show, Bill Mitchell drew his inspiration from the Corvette Sting Ray, which was in the design stage at that time, and a shark which he had seen during a fishing trip off Bimini. Following on from the XP-700, the XP-755 used its transparent roof, equipped with a new rear-view periscope, and its side exhausts, which used bigger pipes to give the impression of fins. A finely-slatted grille covering the headlights, a prominent nose, gill-like housings for the sidelights and turn-signals, and a colour scheme in subtly-graduated shades of grey all combined to make the Shark a true reflection of its namesake.

1962 — Excalibur Hawk Gran Turismo A GT competition prototype on a modified Corvette chassis designed by Brooks Stevens Associates (Brooks Stevens, R. Anderson, J.J. Hughes, G.D. Kelly, B.L. Meyer, D.J. Nutting). The final Excalibur used Studebaker mechanical parts and was one of a number of models designed by this group in association with Studebaker.

1962 — XV '61 A hybrid vehicle with stainless steel bodywork shown by the McLouth Stainless Steel company at the New York Auto Show. Designed as a car with the maximum interior space in the minimum external dimensions it was foreseen as a compact town car which would be connected to a monorail system for long inter-city trips.

95

1962 — Ford Seattle-ite XXI What were Ford's design team dreaming of when they designed this dream car, shown as a 3/8-scale model at the Seattle World's Fair? An extremely long car with four driven steering wheels, it was to be propelled by interchangeable power packages using either fuel cells driving electric motors or 'compact nuclear propulsion devices.' It was to have finger-tip steering and instruments would be replaced by a screen in front of the driver giving not only details of the state of the engine and the car, but also such useful information as the state of the weather and road conditions together with a map display showing exactly where the car was. At the time, Gene Bordinat, Ford's Vice-President in charge of design, said that the car was 'an example of the kind of exploration that can lead to key breakthroughs in automotive design and engineering'.

1961 — Ford Gyron There was no lack of imagination on the part of the Gyron's designers and promoters — nor did they lack a sense of humour. Its specification included a computer system to give automatic control of the driving functions and a viewing system which would give a clear picture of the road ahead regardless of weather conditions. A touch of a button would superimpose speed and estimated time of arrival read-outs on the screen. With only two wheels, positioned fore-and-aft and both driven, the car was to be stabilised by a gyroscope on the move and would be supported by retractable 'training wheels' whilst at rest. All controls were in the centre console, including a 'steering dial' for driving from either seat.

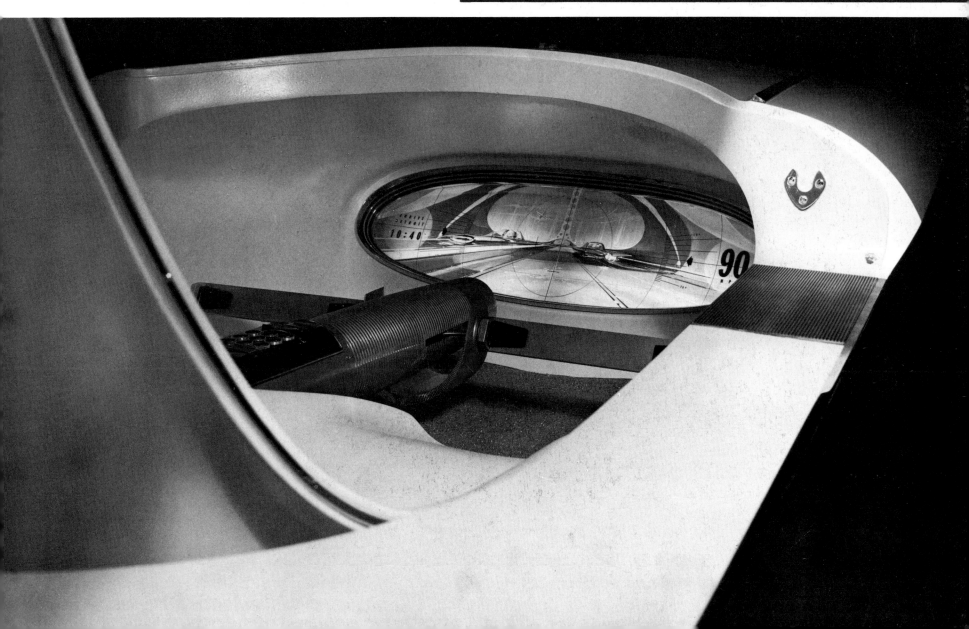

1963 — Chrysler Turbine Those journalists who thought that a revolutionary power-plant required a revolutionary body style were somewhat surprised by the Chrysler turbine car that was unveiled in New York on 14 May 1963. They found it to be a four-seater two-door coupé with restrained styling emphasised by a sombre colour. Only a few details hinted at the presence of a gas-turbine engine, and these were mainly confined to the styling of the exterior trim. For instance, the headlights were surrounded by cowlings with a turbine-blade motif. The same theme was echoed in the wheel-trims, and — in a more pronounced fashion — on the rear lights. On the fascia, a dial showed the speed of the primary turbine and another the temperature of the gas entering the first stage of the turbine. The concept of the flow of gases through a turbine led to the designers' treatment of the headlights and rear end in a manner which suggested the intake and outlet of a jet engine. The men responsible for the Chrysler Turbine — George J. Hubner, chief engineer; Robert Anderson, responsible for production; and Elwood P. Engel, chief stylist, — did not want to create a dream car, but a functional experimental vehicle which would be suitable for use by every-day motorists.

1963 — PF Sigma This project for a safety vehicle was carried out by Pininfarina in collaboration with the staff of the Italian magazine 'Quattroruote' at a time when there was not the same interest in such matters as passive and active safety as there is today. The Sigma provided safe accommodation for its four occupants by use of a passenger compartment surrounded by deformable structures, sliding doors, a well-padded interior, and individual seats provided with head-rests and fitted safety-belts. On the outside, safety demanded a smooth body, free of bumps.

1961 — Ford Volante Castles in the air ? This 'aero-car' was Ford's idea of how the car of the future might look as the 'sixties dawned. According to the designers, 'The triathodyne concept calls for ultra-sophisticated use of the ducted fan principle, employed in a unique manner'. Maybe that's why the Volante never got beyond the stage of a 3/8-scale model and today's cars still use wheels.

1963 — Chevrolet Corvair Testudo Giugiaro is still proud, and rightly so, of the Testudo, which he designed whilst he was at Bertone. On a shortened Corvair Monza Coupé chassis, he created a G.T. car whose low (3 ft 6 ins) and slender lines have not dated in the least. Although such features as the rectangular steering wheel and the hinged windscreen/window/door unit have not found their way on to production cars, there is no doubt that the Testudo did influence the designers of the AMC Pacer, the Mazda RX-7, and the Porsche 924 and 928, which have the same form of retractable headlamps.

1963 — Corvair Super Spyder A spider typical of the Mitchell style of sports car. Based on a Corvair convertible, it married the aggressive lines of the front end, with its chiselled nose and channelled headlamps, to the more flowing and restrained styling evident in the windscreen, rear, and fascia.

1963 — Chevrolet Corvair Monza No other American model of the 'sixties served as a basis for so many stylists' dreams as the ill-starred Corvair, and these two examples from the GM studios are among the wide variety which were produced. The Monza Coupé dispensed with doors, replacing them with a system in which the entire forward part of the passenger compartment hinged forward in one piece. The air-cooled six of the Corvair was mounted ahead of the rear axle and the absence of a transmission tunnel enabled the designers to bring the two front seats close together and thus achieve a spectacular slope to the windscreen and plexiglass side windows. The headlights were covered by two moveable flaps, one opening upwards and one downwards. It was an aesthetically pleasing solution, but not one likely to appeal to the production engineers. At the rear, a venetian blind-type arrangement of slats, adjustable from inside the car, hid the rear window. In the open SS model the headlights were protected by clear, fixed covers. The engine, fed through four carburetters, was this time mounted behind the rear axle. With the two Monza models GM styling showed that it was now in a position to hold its own in the field of 'Grand Touring' cars with the best that Europe — or to be more precise, Turin — could put forward.

1965 — Chevrolet Corvette Mako Shark II Bill Mitchell poses with his personal project, a new dream of a Corvette of the future — the Mako Shark II. Mechanically similar to a production Sting Ray, it was distinguished by a body which was at the same time both voluptuous and aggressive. It also set some kind of record for the number of its power-driven accessories — no less that 17 electric motors were used to activate such goodies as headlamps which were covered by protective flaps, windscreen wipers which retracted beneath the bonnet, a pair of retractable panels in the roof over the front seats (which were fixed, whilst the pedals and wheel were power-adjustable) adjustable head-rests suspended from the roof, moveable slats in the venetian blind which replaced the rear window, an adjustable rear spoiler, a remote-controlled fuel filler and, a final touch, a retractable rear number-plate.

1969 — GM XP 511 Commuter Car This handy little three-wheeler, designed as a vehicle for short urban journeys, is very similar to the Runabout which General Motors presented in its Futurama exhibit at the 1964 New York World's Fair. The Runabout had lines which showed a family resemblance to the Firebird IV and the GM-X and featured a pair of shopping trolleys with retractable wheels which were housed in its rear end. A more roomy vehicle than the XP 511, it had space for two adults in the front and two or three children in the rear.

1964 — GM-X If the Runabout was the GM stylists' idea of a car for the housewives of the future, the GM-X was that perennial designer's dream, the sports car of the next decade — in this case, the 'seventies. According to this view of the cars to come, they would feature access to the cockpit from the rear and enough instrumentation to keep a jet pilot busy. The car was equipped with 21 dials, 31 warning lights, 29 switches, 4 control levers and a cantilever-mounted steering-wheel. To complete the aircraft motif, it also featured retractable air-brakes at the rear.

1964 — Mercer Cobra This open two-seater was commissioned to show the possibilities of using copper and brass for automobile trim. The man entrusted with the job was Virgil M. Exner, who had been working as an independent since 1961. He designed the car in collaboration with his son Virgil Jr., and it was constructed by Sibona & Basano of Turin. The result was a mixture which combined a 'thirties-style radiator flanked by retractable headlights, and flat outrigger wings à la 1911 Mercer, with a Ford Cobra chassis.

1964 — Bugatti 101-C In 1960 the last Bugatti chassis left the Molsheim factory. It was a Type 101, the final Bugatti design, and three years later Ghia of Turin completed work on a body designed by the owner of the chassis, Virgil M. Exner. The American stylist had retained the traditional Bugatti horseshoe radiator, but he surrounded it with the latest rectangular headlights and prominent front wings. At the rear, concave lines contrasted strongly with the frontal treatment. Prominent fuel-caps, chromed outside exhausts, and centre-lock wire wheels all recalled the sporting heritage of the 'pur-sang de l'automobile'.

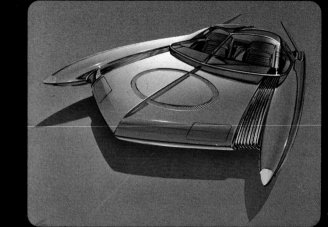

'Preparing for the future — both near and distant — is the mission to which automotive designers are dedicated. Advanced stylists at Ford Motor Company are encouraged to let their imaginations take them into the future, free from the restrictions of what seems possible — or practical — today. In the 'sixties, that was the Ford policy which these sketches illustrated. They show vehicles powered by turbines and solar power cells, land-based or amphibious; all of them further and further removed from the general conception of a car. There is a three-wheeled urban mini-car, a saloon with a track narrower at the front than the back, a sight-seeing bus, a racing car — visions of an utopian future seen through rose-tinted spectacles.

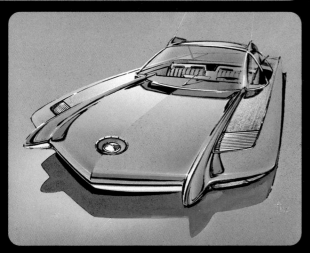

1965 — Alfa Romeo Giulia 1600
A happy marriage between Alfa's space-frame Tubolare racing chassis and subtly rounded bodywork from Pininfarina. The smooth curves of the body are accentuated by the lack of a waist-line and the unusual window shape.

1966 — Dino Berlinetta 206GT
The Ferrari Dino is one of the greatest of Sergio Pininfarina's creations because, in his own words: 'The shape was the starting point for an evolution which even today, fifteen years later, has not reached its final expression. It also represents one of those rare occasions when a dream car became a production reality'.

1966 — De Tomaso Mangusta A▷ newcomer to the automobile zoo, the Mangusta (Mongoose) was built by Ghia with an extremely attractive body designed by Giugiaro on the basis of the 1965 De Tomaso sports. Access to the engine compartment with its 4.7 litre Ford was through the two big panels which formed the smooth rear portion of the roof line. Fitted with tinted plexiglass windows, they were hinged at the centre-line and provided an unrestricted aperture from the door-pillar to the rear bumper.

1966 — Vauxhall XVR Who would have expected a marque so firmly rooted in tradition as Vauxhall to concern itself with futuristic styling exercises? The XVR was designed 'to combine speeds above the 100 mph level with front-rank handling, and a high degree of driver and passenger safety with comfort unpenalised by the very low overall height'. No doubt this was evidence that General Motors did not want to concentrate all its styling activities in the Warren headquarters, but wished to encourage creativity in its European subsiduaries.

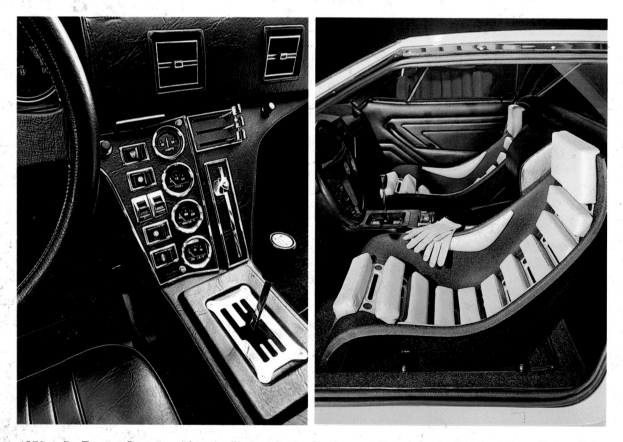

1970 — De Tomaso Pantera After the Mongoose, the Panther was the next animal to lend its name to a Ghia-bodied De Tomaso. This one had a monocoque body with the engine (a 5.7 litre Ford V8) in the classic mid/rear position. In this design Ghia were particularly concerned with combining power, speed, and safety with elegance and comfort. The prototype was equipped with unusual seats composed of horizontal pads supported by a perforated frame, but the limited run of production models had a more traditional Ferrari-style gate change coupled to a five-speed ZF transaxle with limited-slip differential.

112

1958-1966 — Sting Ray Roadster In 1958, Bill Mitchell and his department at GM got hold of an experimental chassis which had been built by Zora Arkus-Duntov, using spares and left-over parts from the Corvette SS. Starting from styling sketches made in 1957 for the new production Corvette — which finally saw the light of day in 1963 as the Sting Ray — Larry Shinoda and Bill Mitchell developed a sports body which was hand-made in fibreglass. The scarlet-painted car became the personal property of Mitchell and he ran it as a private entry in the American sports car racing championships. At the end of the season the Sting Ray, as it was now known, received a new, stronger, body and metallic grey colour scheme. It was in this form that it ran in the Nassau Trophy Race, before being further refined and appearing as a show car at the Chicago Auto Show in 1961. 1962 saw further modifications in the shape of a new bonnet, a passenger windscreen, a 7 litre Mark IV engine, and a new red paint job. Mitchell used it as personal transport in this form until, in 1966, it was returned to its earlier shape and grey colour and was put into store in a General Motors warehouse at Warren, Michigan.

114

1967 — Dino Prototipo Competizione This aerodynamic research exercise by Pininfarina on a mid-engined Dino 206S was more of a design-study than a competition vehicle. It featured singularly rounded lines with a fish-bowl windscreen and 'butterfly' doors hinged at the roof. There was a front wing which could be adjusted for optimum downthrust whilst the car was at rest, but the rear wing was cable-actuated and could be adjusted by the driver on the move. The photograph shows it in the company of another example of well-rounded contemporary styling.

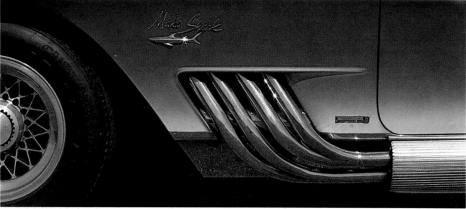

1969 — Chevrolet Corvette Mako Shark I With the loss of its transparent canopy and subsequent transformation into a roadster, the original Shark acquired a new name and a subtle change in style. In the final 1969 version the front end is protected by small bumpers and the bonnet has twin air intakes and outlets catering for the requirements of the 7 litre Mark IV engine. A simpler control panel and a more sombre graduated colour-scheme were other modifications.

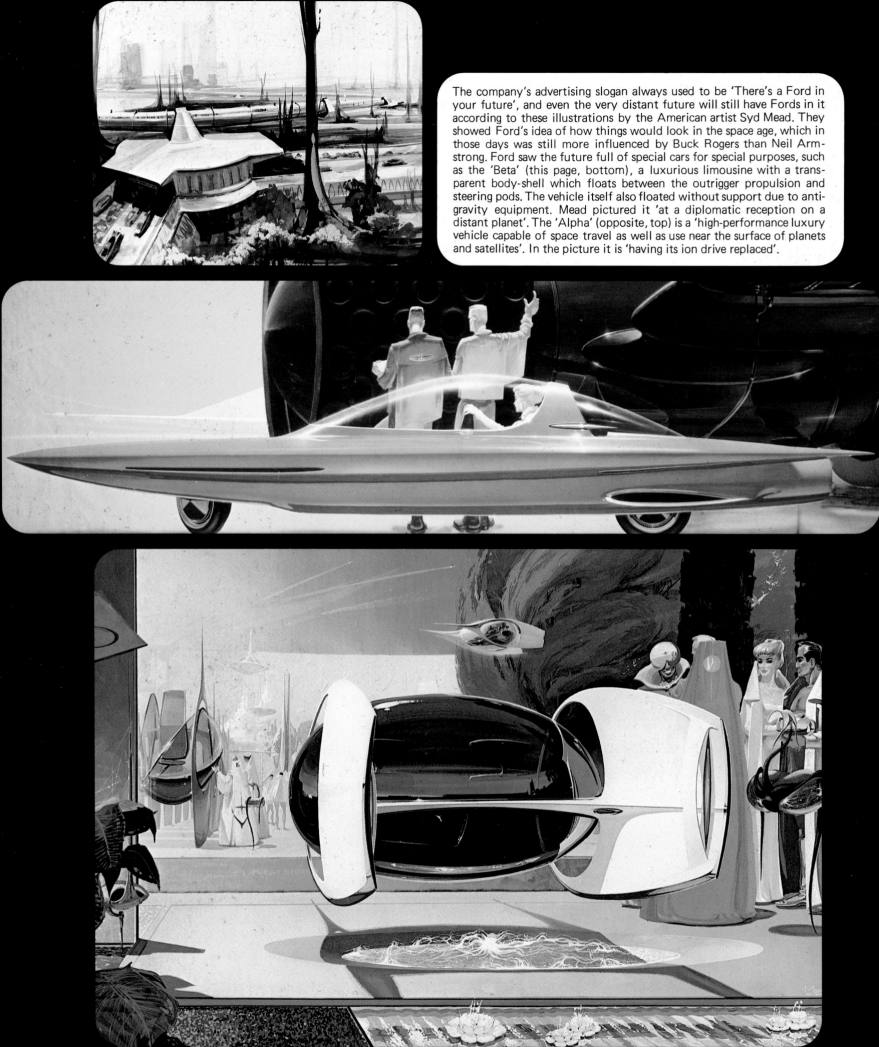

The company's advertising slogan always used to be 'There's a Ford in your future', and even the very distant future will still have Fords in it according to these illustrations by the American artist Syd Mead. They showed Ford's idea of how things would look in the space age, which in those days was still more influenced by Buck Rogers than Neil Armstrong. Ford saw the future full of special cars for special purposes, such as the 'Beta' (this page, bottom), a luxurious limousine with a transparent body-shell which floats between the outrigger propulsion and steering pods. The vehicle itself also floated without support due to antigravity equipment. Mead pictured it 'at a diplomatic reception on a distant planet'. The 'Alpha' (opposite, top) is a 'high-performance luxury vehicle capable of space travel as well as use near the surface of planets and satellites'. In the picture it is 'having its ion drive replaced'.

1967 — Lamborghini Marzal The most striking feature of this prototype, built by Bertone and designed by stylist Marcello Gandini, is the enormous (4.5 square metres 48.4 sq. ft) area of glass, most of it in the windscreen and the unusual doors, hinged at the roof-line and glazed below the waist-line as well as above it. Their gullwing configuration made entrance to the four bucket seats particularly easy. At the rear of the 'glass-house' — which was very well integrated with the rest of the body — was an unique rear window composed of a number of hexagonal panels in a honeycomb configuration. The honeycomb motif was repeated in the fascia panel. The front-end treatment featured a row of six rectangular iodine headlamps in an air-intake bordered and protected by rubber covered blades which formed the bumper. The body was constructed from steel sheet with an aluminium bonnet and was mounted on a chassis derived from that of the Lamborghini Miura. The engine was an in-line six — effectively one half of the Miura's V12 — and was mounted transversally above the rear axle. Like the Miura, the Marzal took its name from a breed of fighting bulls.

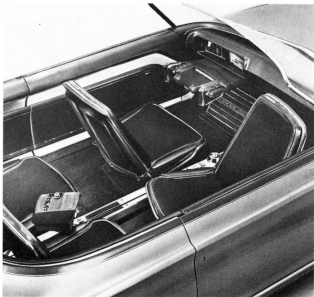

1967 — Chrysler 300 X 'The world's most exciting research vehicle. Mobile proof of what's ahead for you in safety, style, and comfort'. Not too many of those features have arrived yet; amongst them were steering by two retractable handles, a selector dial for the automatic transmission, automatic door-opening and starting using a punched card instead of a key, extra-large adjustable pedals, a TV camera and screen to replace the rear-view mirror, a device for gauging the position of other traffic to assess when it was safe to pass, a TV set for rear-seat passengers, a front passenger seat which swivelled through 180 degrees (for watching television, of course), a speaking clock and, last but certainly not least, 'push-button emptying of ash trays by vacuum action'.

1967 — Chevrolet Astro I With this dream car, which they showed at the New York Auto Show, General Motors put forward yet another solution to the problem of getting into a low-slung sports coupé. This time, not only did the entire rear section of the body work lift up, but the seats were raised by hydraulic lifts at the same time. The fibreglass bodied Astro I was powered by a rear-mounted 2.9 litre Corvair engine. That GM's stylists watched drag races is shown by the full-harness seat belts and their choice of steering-wheel.

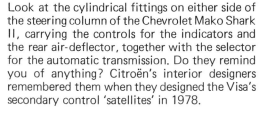

Look at the cylindrical fittings on either side of the steering column of the Chevrolet Mako Shark II, carrying the controls for the indicators and the rear air-deflector, together with the selector for the automatic transmission. Do they remind you of anything? Citroën's interior designers remembered them when they designed the Visa's secondary control 'satellites' in 1978.

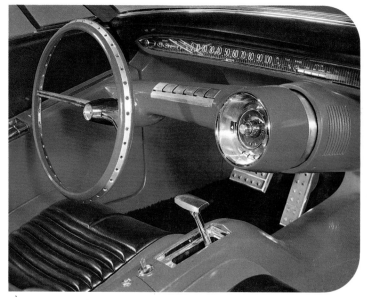

A steering-wheel with a memory was one of the major features of the 1964 Ford Allegro. The wheel was supported by a cantilever arm mounted on a central pivot beneath the instrument panel. Buttons on the arm served to adjust the position of the steering wheel, both up-and-down, and fore-and-aft, together with the position of the assembly carrying the brake and accelerator pedals. To facilitate exit from the car the wheel was pushed upwards and to the right away from the driver. When he got back into the car it was only necessary to push a button and the wheel swung back into position, its memory circuits ensuring that it returned to the right place.

A sumptuous interior smelling of fine leather and rich velvet and complete with a discrete telephone installation. Italian style in a British car : the Bertone-styled Jaguar Ascot of 1977.

1969 — Pontiac Fiero The name means 'fierce', but this two-seater produced by Pontiac for the 1969 New York Show wasn't all that fierce. Racing influence is shown by the wing and the two vestigial head-rests behind the cockpit. It was perhaps a sign of the times that on the threshold of the 'seventies GM's dream cars were no longer far-fetched glimpses of the 'future', but were more like real cars.

1968 — Chevrolet Astro-Vette From the appearance of both the car and the model, one might presume that 1968 was the year of the 'pregnant look'. In the case of the car, the design team which had created the 1968 production Corvette were responsible for the shape. This show vehicle was christened 'Moby Dick' by some ungenerous souls, and it would appear that improved aerodynamics were the aim of the long bonnet and tail, smaller air-intake, and narrow wheels with full covers at the front and fairings at the rear.

1968 — Ferrari Sport Prototipo 250 P5 No less than eight lights stretched across the front of this Pininfarina-styled prototype, linking the bulging front wings. Deep air-outlets in the front deck, massive areas of glass, gull-wing doors, and fascinating glimpses of the engine show the Pininfarina look at its most provocative.

1968 — Ferrari P6 Another Pininfarina design on a Ferrari chassis, this is one of those cars whose balance and serene good looks are apparent from the first glance. It was the starting point for one of the best-known Ferraris of the 'seventies, the Berlinetta Boxer of 1972.

1968 — Alfa Romeo P/33 With less rounded, more aggressive lines than the Ferrari P5, this sports car on the rear-engined Alfa Romeo P33 chassis had a 'roll-bar' which served a triple function. It was at the same time roll-bar, adjustable aileron, and oil-radiator. For the first time, Pininfarina used the wedge shape which had been used for competition cars — most notably in Can-Am types — for some time.

1968 — De Tomaso Mangusta Spider In producing an open version of the Mangusta designed by Giugiaro, Ghia worked hard to retain the lines of the original car whilst refining the front end and finding an original answer to the problem of providing a roll-bar. The screen-pillars are elongated rearwards as far as the rear engine-cover, forming sturdy frames for the side windows, taking the place of the conventional safety hoop and providing a support for the removeable top. Cut-aways at the waistline give the side windows a lozenge shape. The Mangusta Spider's power came from a De Tomaso V8.

1968 — Alfa Romeo 33 Carabo Returning to a theme similar to his Lamborghini Miura of 1966, Bertone was able to style this car more freely, without the same need for practical considerations. Commenting on the design, Sergio Pinintarina described the use of colour and line as 'giving a pure, almost unreal, beauty'. Secret of the beauty was the elongated profile, evocative of an arrow, which gave a feeling of speed, streamlining, and power. The impression was strengthened by the unique treatment of the windscreen and roof shapes, the use of vibrant colour, and the adoption of the special VHR-Gla-verbel glass which could be formed into shapes more flowing than had ever before been possible. The fluorescent colours at front and rear had practical, as well as styling, value, serving to make the car more visible to other road-users. The massive doors swivelled upwards and forwards with the aid

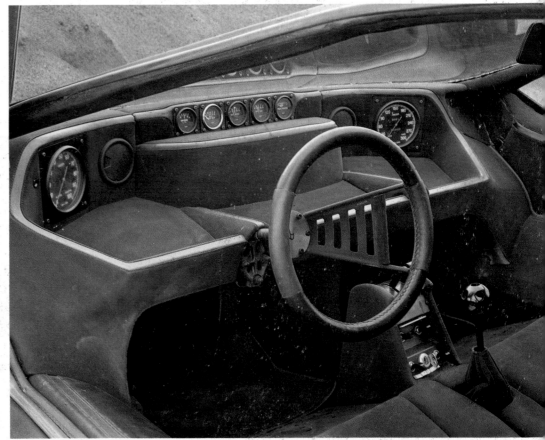

of hydraulic rams, revealing an interior in which stray reflections were eliminated by the use of matt-finished materials in dark colours. The instruments were placed at the lower edge of the windscreen in a position which enabled the driver to see them without taking his eyes from the road ahead. By night, the instrument panel was lit when required in response to pressure on a button on the steering-wheel. In choosing a name for his creation, Bertone drew inspiration from the doors, which resembled a beetle's wing cases, and the dominant metallic green colour of the body. From these elements came the name 'Carabo', Italian for the scarab beetle of the ancient Egyptians.

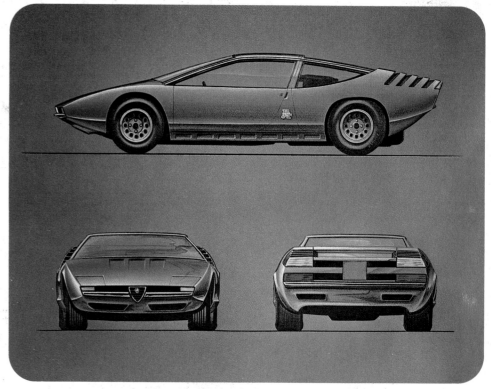

1969 — Alfa Romeo Iguana In 1968, after four years at Ghia, Giorgio Giugiaro, together with Aldo Mantovani and Luciano Bosio, formed Ital Design SIRP (Societa Industrial per la Realisazione di Prototipi) at Moncalieri, outside Turin. The Iguana was the successor to the Bizzarini Manta displayed one year earlier at the 1968 Turin Auto Show. It took the form of an attractive design-study on an Alfa P33 Stradale chassis and was intended for small-scale production. A notable feature was the sharp angle of the front end — steeper even than in the preliminary sketches — and the highly individual line formed by the relationship between the front and rear panels. The interior was trimmed in grained materials which echoed the texture of the brushed steel finish of the body.

1969 — Autobianchi Runab
designers' fantasy for a be
real technical interest? No
inspection of this mid/rear-
reveals it to be a much more
tion which served as a basis
of 1972. As had become the
and chief stylist Gandini p
into creating an original inter
repeated in the seats, steer
panel and even the gear-leve

1969 — Abarth 2000 Unlike the other Italian stylists, Pininfarina did not choose the names for his creations from the realms of zoology. However, this prototype, half-way between a racer and a dream car, could very well have been christened Testudo in honour of the tortoise-like form of its general appearance — and particularly in view of the rear, aft of the roof with its lateral air-intakes.

1969 — Mercury Super Spoiler The profusion of wings which flourished on the Formula 1 cars of 1968 could not fail to have its effect on American dream cars. The spoiler which dressed up this canary yellow Mercury had no aerodynamic effect but it did offer a measure of decorative protection to this creation based on the Cyclone and Cyclone GT production models.

1969 — Ford Super Cobra An enormous dragster-style air-intake to feed a greedy engine, headlights set behind slats which echo those of the 'venetian blind' at the rear, clumsy bodywork: Ford's stylists were passing through a period where imagination was not their strong point.

1969 — Chrysler Concept 70X An old idea brought up to date: the doors were mounted on parallelogram hinges and opened alongside the body protruding only 38 cm (1 ft 3 ins) when open. An innovation was an ultra-sonic device which was mounted at the rear and swept an area of 180 degrees to a distance of 15 metres (50 ft). The presence of any object in this field was signalled to the driver by means of a red light mounted in the rear-view mirror. Maybe the designers felt it was necessary to protect the long fibreglass body, inspired by that of the Plymouth Fury, from accidental shortening.

1969 — Ford Mark II Dual Cowl Phaeton
'A favourite body style of movie stars and millionnaires of the thirties lives again in this most recent of Ford's dream cars'. What they didn't mention was that those famous Dual Cowl Phaetons with their twin windscreens had four doors whilst this camouflaged Lincoln Continental had only two. No-one seemed to bother, however, as it made its debut on Hollywood's Wilshire Boulevard where, forty years earlier, fans could spot Gary Cooper, Tom Mix, or maybe Gloria Swanson at the wheel of a torpedo-bodied sports tourer.

1969 — Toyota EX III This coupé, with its shark's mouth air-intake, smooth undertray, and generously-distributed windows, was one of the first Japanese experimental cars. Toyota presented it at the Tokyo Auto Show at the same time as the EX I, the prototype of a GT car which was comparable to the best work of the Italian stylists. It is interesting to note that although other Japanese marques called on foreign stylists from time to time (Mazda and Bertone, Daihatsu and Vignale, Datsun and Pininfarina), Toyota carried out its own styling work.

1969 — Plymouth Duster I A powerful and over-elaborate version of the Plymouth Road Runner equipped with a 7 litre 426 Hemi V8 developing 425 hp. Four moveable flaps — two situated on the rollbar, and two let into the body, level with the fillercaps — acted as airbrakes. The choice of name was ambiguous — was it a Duster that would clean up the opposition or, in its naval sense, a Duster signalling the arrival of a fleet of similarly way-out vehicles?

1969 — AMX/2 This superb mid/rear-engined coupé is not the work, as one might think, of a top Turin stylist, but of Richard 'Dick' Teague, head of styling at America's smallest manufacturer, American Motors, founded in 1954 by Nash-Kelvinator and Hudson.

1969 — Buick Century Cruiser Take an old dream car — not too old of course, something like a 1964 Firebird IV will do fine. Change a few of the details, give it a new paint job, and select a new name — something futuristic for preference. Garnish with an attractive model and serve to as many people as you can get on to your stand at the New York Auto Show.

1969 — Pontiac Cirrus If the recipe ▷ worked for Buick, there's no reason why it shouldn't work for Pontiac. In their case the slightly stale model was a 1964 GM-X Stiletto. A new front end, new paint, and a new model in a mini-skirt did the trick for them.

1969 — Hurricane RD 001 Holden, General Motors' Australian subsidiary, were responsible for this rear-engined coupé. It had a roof/doors/windscreen unit which swung forward for access, and a tilting steering wheel which swung out of the driver's way for easy entrance to a cockpit which contained a TV screen in place of a rear-view mirror. Only the big boot-sized pedals show original Australian, rather than second-hand American, thinking.

1969 — Opel CD Another vehicle with a single-piece 'greenhouse' which pivoted forward for entry, particularly notable for the size of the single piece of glass which forms the windscreen and side-windows. Based on Opel Diplomat mechanical components, this lively yet elegant design was carried out under the control of Charles M. Jordan, now chief stylist at GM, during his period at Russelsheim.

142

1969-1973 — Chevrolet Corvette 4-Rotor or 'AeroVette' Derived from the XP 882 prototype, a mid-engined GT coupé with a chassis developed under the control of Zora Arkus-Duntov that was first shown at the New York Auto Show in 1970, the AeroVette was fitted with two twin-rotor rotary engines coupled together with a capacity equivalent to 9.5 litres and producing 350 hp at 7000 rpm, the largest Wankel engine ever mounted in an automobile. The extremely attractive body was the work of Charles M. Jordan and introduced a new style in gullwing doors, hinged both at the roof centreline and the top of the window. The cockpit, the product of Chevrolet's foremost interior stylists, used digital instrument displays. Soon after its appearance at the Paris Show in 1973, the AeroVette's rotary engine was replaced by a V8 for the sake of simplicity.

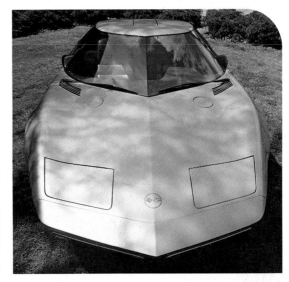

1969 — Chevrolet Astro III Wheels: three. Seats: two. Engine: one (turbine). Purpose: experimental. Style: spaceship. Utilisation: static display at shows. Descendant: none.

1969 — Alfa Romeo 33 Although following the general lines of the 512 Ferrari, this Pininfarina design was more suited to road use, with such legal necessities as headlamps and parking lights. The cockpit was equipped to seat two people comfortably and an embryonic boot was squeezed into the rear to take a limited amount of luggage.

1970 — Ferrari 512S Modulo Shown at the Geneva and Turin Motor Shows and the Osaka World Fair, the Pininfarina Modulo excited the interest of all who saw it. Never before had there been a car with such an unusual shape, such perfect proportions, or such power to give the impression of movement. The body was constructed from two shells joined at the waistline and surrounded by a moulding which formed the mounting for the bumpers and rear lights. The forward part of the roof slid forward on rails to reveal a cockpit with twin spherical housings for controls and fresh-air vents. The vehicle was a superb example of how new techniques could be combined in a style which was at the same time simple yet revolutionary in its approach.

1965 — Plymouth VIP An impressive show car from Chrysler which was displayed at the Chicago Auto Show on their top-of-the-line Imperial chassis. The T roof supported two panels of photo-sensitive glass which slid forward from their hiding places in the boot. The glass was designed to become darker as the sun got brighter until the point at which the sun was so bright and the glass so dark that it would be deemed a good idea to remove the protection the glass provided and bask in the sunshine — such is the perversity of human nature. Other innovations were a radio-telephone, stereo tape-recorder, and TV rear-view mirror — classed as an innovation because it could also receive normal programmes.

1970 — VW Porsche 914/6 Tapiro This, the fourth prototype produced by the Ital Design partnership, is the favourite of Giorgio Giugiaro. The wedge shape, large areas of glass, aggressive profile, and the way in which the windscreen hardly breaks the sharp angle of the nose are all favourite themes of the Turin stylist and combine together magnificently on this standard VW-Porsche platform. The windscreen supports, the doors, the transparent engine-compartment covers, and the rear panel are all joined by the central spine to form a cohesive whole.

149

1970 — Lancia Stratos Prototipo 'From the stylist's point of view, the ideal format for a performance car is the mid/rear-engine configuration. It permits him to create a line which is at the same time aerodynamically efficient and aesthetically pleasing, and the lack of bulky components at the front of the vehicle gives him the ability to design a low, wind-cheating nose'. The truth of this proposition is well shown by this Bertone creation on Lancia Fulvia 1.6 HF mechanicals. The philosophy which led to this design started in 1966 with the Miura and continued through the Marzal, Panther, Carabo, Runabout, and Urraco. It now reached the stage where the only glass areas of the car were the trapezium-shaped windscreen and the small side-windows — of which only the top sections were moveable. Entry to the 33 inch high car was effected by stepping onto the panel ahead of the lift-up windscreen/door and climbing into the car's 'mouth', grasping the steering-wheel and column — which folded away automatically as the door was opened — for support.

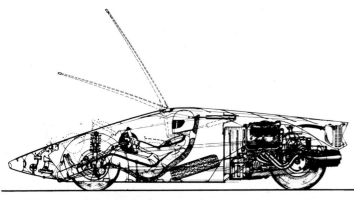

1969 — Ferrari 512S Berlinetta Speciale Pininfarina built this model on the chassis of the first Ferrari 512, derived from the company's Can-Am racer. The result was an impressive vehicle whose wedge shape resulted from collaboration with the Turin Polytechnic. A single unbroken line joined the chisel nose and the high tail which was chopped off sharply behind the perforated cover over the 4.9 litre V12 engine. Front and rear views gave a much bulkier impression than that given by the slim profile.

Now here is a car that would merit the 'Ant-Eater' label that Giugiaro gave to his VW-Porsche prototype. However, such a name would be out of the question, for this 100,000 dollars custom car was specially built to appear in and publicise a TV cartoon series featuring the Pink Panther — any other animal references would have amounted to zoological overkill. The luxurious interior contained a TV set, telephone, numerous vanity mirrors, and a lemonade dispenser (it was a children's cartoon). The driver, perched forward in the nose, did not share these comforts but at least he was kept warm by the Oldsmobile V8 just behind his seat. In any case, with 500 hp in a vehicle just under 26 ft long, lemonade might be too strong.

1970 — Lamborghini Urraco Dream car or production machine? It is difficult to draw the line when faced with a model such as this, which is made exclusive by its performance, price, and extremely limited production. Bertone introduced this small Lamborghini coupé with its 2.5 litre V8 engine at the 1970 Turin show, but it is not a car you will see too often in your local supermarket parking area.

1970 — Ford Tridon A study by Ford's research staff on a Thunderbird chassis which looked at new ideas in shapes — the 'three element' nose, faired-in rear wheels, recessed rear-window, and clear plastic roof panel; in materials — tinted glass, plastic bumpers; in colour schemes — the windows were all tinted to complement the body colour; and in interior arrangements — a central console, synthetic lambswool upholstery, and a telephone for busy jaws.

154

1968 — Dodge Charger III Dodge publicity at the time said: 'A bold, new imaginative experimental car from Dodge designed to significantly diminish the distance between the will of man and the response of the machine. Its every feature is aimed at providing instant response to the desires and commands of its two occupants — whether for comfort, convenience, enormous acceleration, tremendous speed, or for long-distance, mile-eating cruising'.

1970 — Mazda RX 500 Star attraction at the seventeenth Tokyo Motor Show was this car from the research and design staff of the Toyo Kogyo company. Designed as a mobile test-bed for high-speed safety and the use of plastics in automobile bodies, it had a rotary engine mounted ahead of the rear axle. According to the factory, the 1100 lb car was capable of 125 mph. A series of multi-coloured lights in the rear end indicated whether the car was accelerating, braking or running at constant speed. The body, more attractive from the front than when seen in side-view, was typical of contemporary styling trends in the field of mid-engined two-seaters.

1970 — Mazda EX 005 Shown at the same time as the RX 500, this interesting project for a town car utilised a hybrid power plant in which a constant-speed rotary engine charged a battery, which in turn provided the power for an electric motor. Providing space for four passengers, the EX 005 was constructed from three plastic components (the platform, interior and removeable canopy) and featured a single manual control between the front seats which took the place of accelerator, brake, and steering-wheel.

1970 – Nissan 126 X This Japanese dream car had a wedge shape, a cockpit canopy which tilted forward, and a side-window shape which stands comparison with some Ghia designs of later in the decade. The slots along the bonnet's centre-line were not for cooling purposes, but housed red, yellow, and green lights which lit up according to whether the car was accelerating, braking, or running at steady speed. Also to be found at the back end of the cover over the rear-mounted 3 litre six-cylinder engine.

1971 – Nissan 216 X This coupé was derived from a four-seat safety vehicle on which Nissan was working at the time. The proposed powerplant was a transverse-mounted four cylinder unit of 2 litres capacity. The massive bumpers were designed to extend automatically when the car was in motion, both front and rear units protruding by just under six inches. In the event of an impact, air-bags would automatically inflate in the passenger compartment to protect the occupants. The hump on the roof housed the optical components of a rear-view periscope.

1965-1968 — Reventlow Formula Libre X-15 A road car? With Bill Mitchell, nothing is impossible — let him tell the story in his own words: 'I visited Lance Reventlow's shop in California just after his retirement from racing. His Scarab and my Sting Ray had many duels together, and he usually came off better because the Scarab had disc brakes on all four wheels. Then he went overseas on Formula One challenges that proved rather fruitless. Then he tried to promote the Formula Libre series which had been popular in England. This never developed in North America. When I was out visiting Lance to acquire one of his top men, Warren Olson, to take care of my show cars, he said to me: 'Do you want this car?' — which was his Formula Libre racer with a Chevrolet 350 engine and Hilborn fuel injection. I said 'Yes' and he sent it to me. I wanted to change the car from a racing car to a street car and that's why I restyled it and modified it for street use. I sure had a hell of a lot of fun with it and as you can imagine, everyone who saw it wished that it was theirs. I had a regular 350 Chevrolet engine with three carburettors installed. The shield over the carbs acted as a lock when I left the car unattended — I merely lifted the top off when I started the car. It was a lot of fun. I drove it for three years but when all the ballyhoo about safety started I returned it to its original condition and sent it back to Lance. Just prior to his untimely death he gave the car to Briggs Cunningham who now has it in his museum'. 'It was a lot of fun'. — Nice touch of understatement there, Mr Mitchell.

1967 — Mercury Wrist-Twist Well, look at it this way: It did give a good view of the instruments. Another example of the 'Let's-replace-a-simple-component-with-a-complicated-one' syndrome.

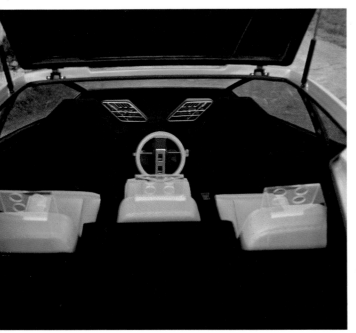

1974 — Ford Coins A Ghia project designed by Filippo Sapino and Tom Tjaarda and based on a view of what a future Capri-type car would look like. It had three seats with a central driving position and entry to the passenger compartment was through a single door at the rear.

1979 — Volvo 343 Tundra The electronic instruments of this Bertone design are certainly attractive, but whether their graphic display of information would be easy for a driver to read is open to question.

1979 — Ford Probe 1 The idea which Giorgio Giugiaro put forward in the fascia panel of his Maserati Boomerang is here seen as brought up to date by Ford stylists at Dearborn with the addition of an array of illuminated digital displays, a variety of switches and keyboards for a couple of computers.

Xpak 400 Air Car (left) An experimental air-cushion vehicle built for the American magazine 'Car Craft' by the king of the customisers, George Barris — who is of course an inhabitant of Hollywood. This 53 year-old Californian has for many years specialised in the design and construction of unique custom cars for films and television, as well as personal transportation for some of their more extrovert stars. Although his products may be fantastic, his skill and production methods enjoy a high reputation, and both Ford and GM have entrusted construction of some of their dream car projects to him. This car was a scale model some eight feet wide, radio-controlled and capable of operating on land or water.

Turbo-Sonic Another Barris creation (above left) for a TV series entitled 'Tom Jones's Garage a Go-Go'. Propelled by a turbine engine (so the story goes) it had disc brakes, air brakes, a braking parachute — and only three wheels. Now you know why it needed all those brakes.

Stiletto (Above) An exhibition vehicle designed by Detroit stylist Gene Baker and built by Ron Gerstner on a space-frame chassis. It was powered by a Corvair engine and was built to the order of an executive of a car-show promoting company.

Land Sea Air Car Another Barris production (left), this capsule with its retractable wings represented a vision of a car which would be equally at home on land, sea, or air.

1970 — Mercedes-Benz C 111 A sports coupé of such style and comfort that even the most demanding of wealthy enthusiasts would be happy to own it, a vehicle whose limits of speed and road-holding were so high that only a professional driver could explore them, and a technologically-complex 'rolling laboratory' such as only the upper echelons of the world's motor industry have the re-sources — both technical and financial — to construct; the C 111 was all these things. This second example of the car differed from its predecessor, announced the previous year, in its body — which had new front air-intakes and cut-aways in the roof at the rear — and a new four-rotor Wankel engine which replac-ed the triple-rotor unit of the earlier model. The new engine had a chamber volume of 2.4 litres, making it the equivalent of a 4.8 litre engine of normal configuration. It pro-duced 350 hp at 7000 rpm and gave accel-eration figures of 0 to 60 mph in a fraction under 4.8 seconds.

1971 — Alfasud Caimano Designed by Giugiaro and built by Ital Design, this angular coupé was very futuristic in its lines and featured the kind of swivelling windscreen/doors unit which Giugiaro had used in the Corvair Testudo in 1963. Unique wheel styling and a tubular instrument panel with graphic display were amongst its novel features.

1971 — Lamborghini LP 500 Countach In the dialect of Italy's Piedmont, 'count-ach' is an expression of astonishment and amazement. Such feelings were much in evidence when Bertone unveiled this Gandini-designed prototype with a rear-mount-ed V12 Lamborghini 4.9 litre engine disposed longitudinally (the 'LP' designation comes from the Italian 'longitudinale posteriore'). The gearbox was mounted in front of the engine and protruded between the seats, and the doors opened upwards and forwards in a similar manner to those on the Carabo.

Starting in 1973, the Countach was produced in very limited numbers. Production cars varied from the prototype in a number of details, the most important of these being improved cooling brought about by the placing of NACA ducts in the body sides, faired-in air-ducts at the rear of the cockpit, and intakes in the rear wings. Other major changes were the adoption of a tubular chassis, a reduction in engine size to 4 litres, revised rear wings and lamps, and a new interior.

1971-1972 — Maserati Boomerang In this coupé Giorgio Giugiaro was attempting to create 'the ultimate sports car' in terms of contemporary technology and styling. Its wedge shape, with the windows and air vents forming flights for the arrow of the waistline, suggested speed and movement. A car that really did look as though it was doing a hundred miles per hour when it was standing still. First shown by Ital Design at the Turin show as a mock-up, it became a rolling prototype some months later on a basis of Maserati Bora mechanical parts, with the 4.7 litre V8 engine ahead of the rear axle. The unique instrument panel position was designed by Giugiaro with visibility and safety in the case of a frontal impact in mind. All the major instruments were gathered together in an oversize steering-wheel centre. The steering-column itself was split and transmitted its movements to the steering mechanism by means of a chain-drive.

166

1972 — BMW Turbo A prestige-building 'visiting card' for the Bavarian performance car-builder, the Turbo succeeded in combining a number of elements which do not always go well together. Firstly, it was an extremely attractive car, secondly, it was very practical in the way it proposed a number of valid answers to problems in the fields of active and passive safety, and thirdly it was the precursor of a production model — albeit in small numbers. The French designer Paul Bracq, head of the design staff at BMW from 1970 to 1974, was responsible for the styling, which was conceived 'with a view to making the car a feasible proposition for series production while at the same time retaining an originality of line'. Passive safety was very much in mind and the car had front and rear deformable structures, massive self-coloured 'bumper' mouldings for the nose and tail, no less than three impact-absorbing universal joints in the steering-column, a robust roll-over bar in the cockpit roof, clear and legible instrumentation, form-fitting seats, and an unusual high-visibility colour scheme in tones of red and orange. To provide active safety there was an anti-skid braking system, an aerodynamic form designed to assist road-holding, good weight distribution, and a turbo-charged 2 litre engine.

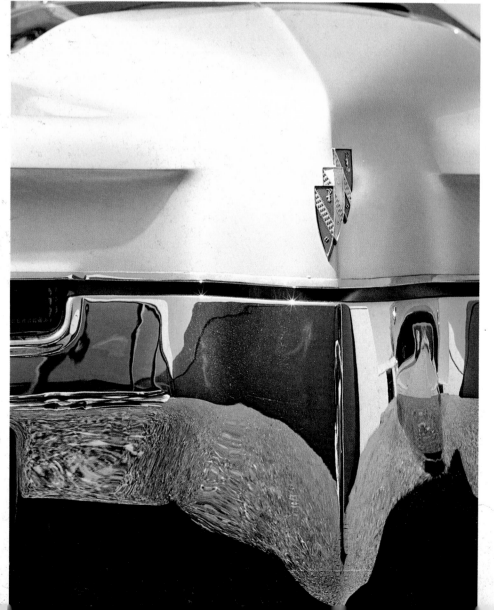

1972 — Buick Riviera Silver Arrow III This stylish show-car differed only in detail from the 1971 production version of the Riviera, but the detailing had a profound effect on the look of the car. The grille was replaced by one with rectangular apertures, 'banana' over-riders were fitted, the bonnet was more pointed, cornering lamps were fitted at the front, there were two air-outlets above the rear window, the sides of the window itself were shaped to follow the contours of the rear deck, the rear quarter lights were also shaped to follow the wing line, the rear lights were recessed in the bumpers and over-riders, and the boot lid had two sculptured depressions to emphasise the lines of the wings and fast-back. Inside, the trim was all coloured silver to reflect the car's name. Maybe William L. Mitchell was thinking of this car when he said to us in early 1980: 'The dictionary describes "vogue" as a form of temporary usage. A good design lasts forever and becomes a classic. A poor design sits around to haunt you'.

1973 — Chevrolet Corvette 2-Rotor The second rotary-engined Corvette, this prototype was originally named the Chevrolet GT. In the minds of its creators it was seen firstly as a replacement for the Opel GT, and later on as a Corvette successor — the world's first volume-production mid-engined sports car. The body, similar in size to that of a Ferrari Dino, was made in only twelve weeks by Pininfarina. It was given its first public showing, alongside the AeroVette, at the Frankfurt Motor Show in September 1973. The headlamp treatment, with the lamps set into deep channels in the sloping nose, was to become a feature of GM production cars, notably the Chevrolet Monza 2 + 2, two years later.

1973 — Pontiac Phantom Speaking in January 1980, William L. Mitchell said of this car: 'Realising that, with the energy crisis and other considerations, the glamour car would not be around for long, I wanted to leave a memory at General Motors of the kind of cars I love. This car represents the line, shape and image I love in a motor car — sleek and racy with no severe, boxy, hard lines. A V windshield, a long hood coming through the windshield as in the 'thirties — clean and fast. Nostalgically elegant with modern headlights and flush glass in the doors. The doors hinge on the rear pillar for easy entrance and are electrically bolted for safety. This was designed for the new Seville chassis with front-wheel-drive and independent rear suspension. Maybe the days of these elegant cars will return — we can dream anyway'. In line with Mitchell's enthusiasm for performance, the Phantom was also designed to have fierce acceleration. The fact that it would have a 'gas-guzzling' fuel consumption to match explains why it was the car which marked the end of an era.

171

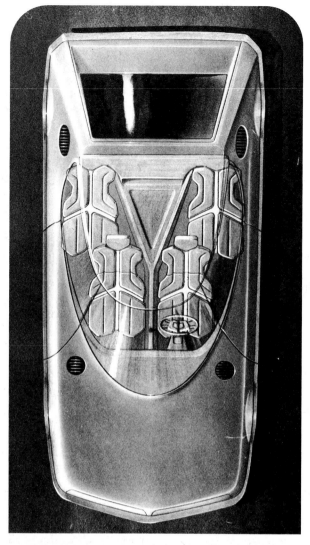

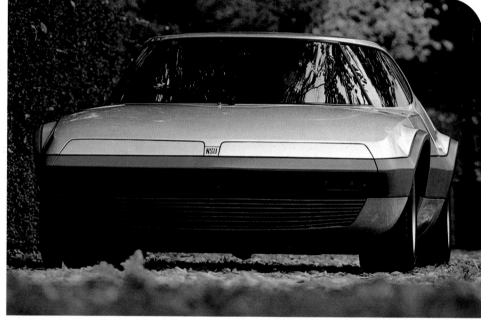

1973 — Audi-NSU Trapeze A mid-engine configuration is generally accepted as being the ideal one to give the kind of performance and handling qualities which a modern GT car should provide, but the problem is how to provide accommodation for four people without compromising their comfort and safety. Bertone's solution was to arrange the seats in a trapezium-shaped configuration — hence the car's name — and to use an engine of compact overall dimensions, the Wankel rotary unit from the NSU Ro 80. The front seats were as close together as possible, and the rear passengers were split by the engine housing. Positioning the seats in this manner gave rear seat passengers excellent leg-room and access as well as having a beneficial aerodynamic effect on the shape of the cockpit.

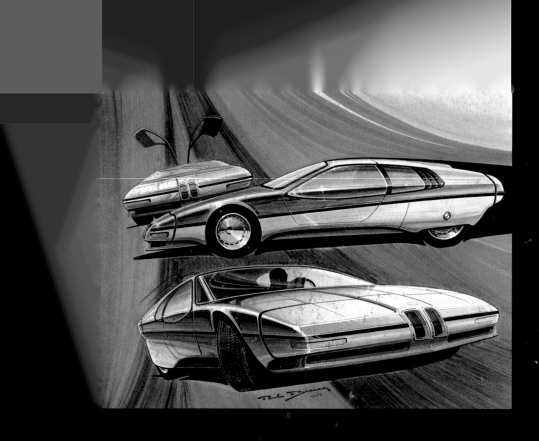

Throughout his career in the automobile industry, Paul Bracq has devoted his leisure time to those same cars which filled his working hours. It is a career which has led from studying coachbuilding in his native France to his present position as head of interior design at Peugeot and which included along its path a period with Charbonneau, a French coachbuilding company, ten years with Daimler-Benz' research department, work with the Brissoneau and Lotz design partnership, and four years as head of design for BMW. During his stay in Munich, Bracq was responsible for, among other cars, the trend-setting BMW Turbo. As a relaxation from designing cars he paints them, and in the selection of his work reproduced here one can sense his appreciation of the automobile as an art form.

1974 — Studio Cr 25 The connection between the car, the girl, and the camels is difficult to guess. One theory is that the picture was taken for a newspaper competition in which readers were asked to place them in ascending order of drag co-efficient. The winner was the car, which Pininfarina had smoothed down to achieve a figure of only 0.25. Built with a view to construction on the mechanical elements of a Ferrari, this experimental body demonstrated the results of wind-tunnel research. Among its aerodynamic aids were air-brakes situated behind the windows and bumpers designed to act as spoilers.

1974 — Lamborghini Bravo The stamp of Bertone and Marcello Gandini is all over this prototype based on the Lamborghini Urraco. Typical of the style is the way in which functional elements such as the front air intakes, the rear quarter lights, and the rear window are treated as decorative features and integrated into the overall design scheme. Cleanliness of design is certainly next to godliness at Bertone, and the line of this car has been further cleansed by the way in which the use of tinted glass and an almost invisible screen pillar has minimised the visual 'break' between the front and side areas of glass. The name, besides being an internationally recognised exclamation of approbation, is another of the Lamborghini/Bertone references to bull-fighting: 'Bravo' is the name given to a particularly brave fighting bull.

1975 — Chevrolet Super Monza A modest dream for a year of crisis, a show car derived from the Monza 2+2 (or from the Oldsmobile Starfire, its almost identical twin). A 'droop-snoot' nose, flared wheel arches, a rear spoiler and an asymmetric bonnet air-intake all said 'performance'. And just in case you didn't get the message, a decal on the bonnet said it even louder.

1975 — Alfa Romeo Eagle A daring ▷ interior, with electric-blue velvet upholstery, digital instruments, and touch-control switches, contrasted with the restrained body styling of this convertible which Pininfarina built on the basis of an Alfetta GT.

1976 — L'Aiglon The longest (23 feet) and most extravagant of the cars designed by Luigi Colani, a German of Italian extraction whose fertile imagination has given birth to a multitude of creations not only in the realm of land, sea, and air transport, but also in the field of interior decoration and the plastic arts. He described this car as his view of how sports cars would have looked by 1940 if the war had not intervened. This is perhaps the only point in favour of the war.

1976 — Alfa Romeo Navajo Built on the Alfa Romeo T33 sports racing car chassis, with its centrally mounted flat 12 engine, this two-seater coupé was described by Bertone as a study in using aerodynamics as a means to increasing adhesion rather than pure speed. It was this which led to the use of front and rear wings which varied their angles in relation to the car's speed by means of a special patented linkage. A unique feature was the manner in which the headlamps, mounted at the front of the wings, swung out sideways to the operating position. The digital instrument panel display was capable of showing not only basic information on the car's operating conditions such as road and engine speeds, temperatures, etc, but also graphic displays of speed against braking distance etc.

1976 — Ferrari Rainbow So named because of its potential for use in rain or sun, the Rainbow was a design exercise by Bertone in which the problems of a convertible car were approached from a new angle. Instead of a fabric hood, a steel top covered the occupants in inclement weather and slid back mechanically to stow itself behind the seats when the climate improved. The Rainbow was featured in the 1979 Christmas catalogue of the Marshal Field chain stores as one of the specially selected gifts for the man or woman who has everything. It would be interesting to know whether any were sold in this way. With a two-hundred-thousand-dollar price tag, and an eighteen month delivery delay, it seems unlikely.

OUR CHRISTMAS STARS

A. FERRARI 308 GT RAINBOW: A Marshall Field's first, and ours alone in all the world. Bertone's custom-made show body on a Dino 308 GT4 chassis. A one-of-a-kind car with famous Bertone avant-garde styling. An engineering marvel, the convertible top slides behind the seat while the skylight becomes a unique rear window/windscreen. For details and specifications, call (312) 781-5354. 200,000.00 (F.O.B. Turin, Italy. U.S. emission and safety required equipment not included. 18 months delivery.)

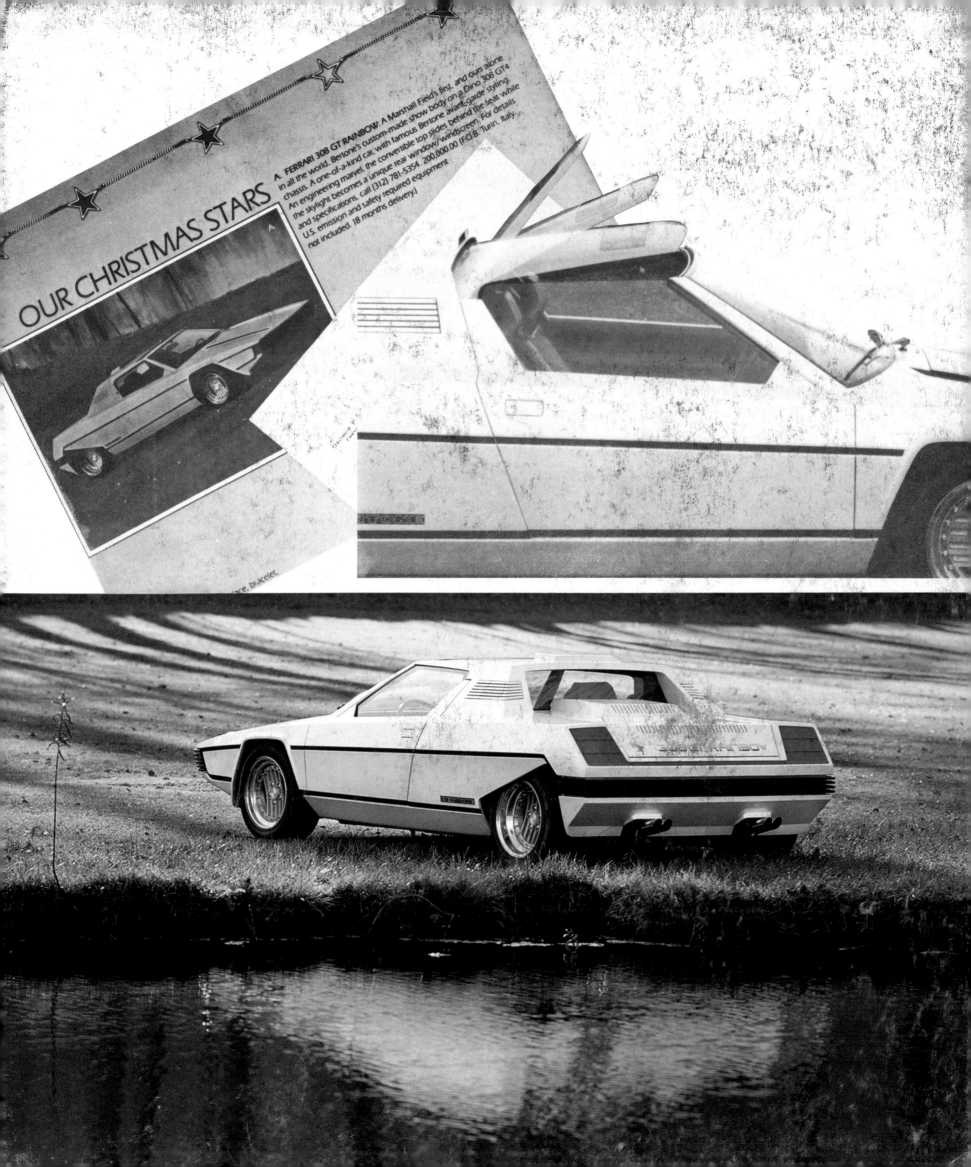

1978 — Ford Megastar II In 1967 Ghia was bought by the American Rowan Controller Company and Alejandro de Tomaso was named as its new president. Three years later, Rowan sold 80 per cent of its shares to Ford and the rest to de Tomaso. In 1972 he, in turn, sold his shares to Ford. So it was that in 1973 Ghia came under total Ford control and became the company's European centre for advanced styling studies. It retained its own name, however, and in fact Ford began to use the name for various luxury versions of its production cars. Filippo Sapino, who had worked at Ghia from 1960 to 1967, headed the operation. The Megastar II, based on the Ford Fiesta, was the successor to the first car of the same name, a four-door estate car built in 1977 on a Granada platform. It followed the general styling trend of the earlier car with large rounded areas of glass cutting low into the doors at the sides and another big window in the high-set rear end. The expansive glazed areas were of dark-tinted glass and contrasted strongly with the metallic-grey bodywork and the touches of colour provided by the rear lights and the band which ran round the lower portions of the body.

1976-1977 — Ford Corrida Ghia presented this car at the Turin Show in 1976, basing it on the floor-pan of the Fiesta which had been introduced only two months previously. The Corrida was equipped with gullwing doors hinged at the roof and waist lines, headlamps disguised by flat covers, and a boot which extended back horizontally. The new Ghia style was evident in the elongated lines, the angular profile, the breaking up of large flat surfaces by fine trim and shut-lines, and the use of tinted glass to further define the glazed areas.

fiesta 2 pass.

1978-1979 — Studies for an ideal aerodynamic form
In 1976 Pininfarina was approached by the Italian National Research Council (CNR) to collaborate in studies to determine the ideal aerodynamic shape for a 4/5 seater car of moderate engine size. A lengthy series of experiments gave rise to the creation of a full-size model (above) which, by means of a shape which owed everything to smooth aerodynamics and nothing to automobile practicalities, achieved the incredibly low drag coefficient of 0.161. The second phase of the work was to adapt the shape to include those items considered indispensible for a road car (lights, wipers, rear-view mirrors, air-intakes, etc.) and to make the ideal into something more closely resembling a useable road vehicle. This gave rise to the model shown at the left which, although unkindly dubbed the 'banana car' by some, had a very creditable drag co-efficient of 0.23.

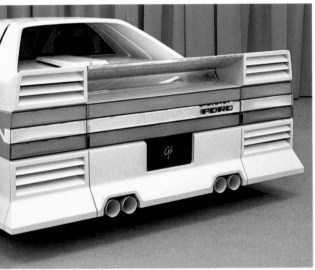

1978 — Action A design study for a competition car to be powered by a Ford DFV 3 litre V8 engine, this vehicle featured a wide front spoiler which swept back over the front wheels to form a wide skirt which completely enclosed the rear wheels. Only just over three feet high, it was, according to Filippo Sapino, the man responsible for its design at the Ford-owned Ghia studio, intended for use 'as a basis for a research programme (to) pursue a study of its aerodynamic principles which could then be applied to the standard production family sedan' — sentiments expressed by Ford spokesmen throughout the period covered by this book.

1978-1979 — Jaguar XJ 12 Pininfarina's most recent work is a tasteful combination of traditional and current lines with future trends. In this car, the classic rounded lines of the D and E Types have obviously influenced the thinking, as have the lessons learnt in the wind-tunnel while the aerodynamic forms were being developed.

1978 — Lancia Sibilo In many of his prototypes, Bertone made the glazed areas an important part of the functional and aesthetic design. In the Sibilo (a name created from the words 'solid' and 'mobile') he attempted to achieve a complete integration of glass and metal by using tinted glass in shapes that would combine with the metal areas to create a homogeneous overall form. The lay-out of the interior showed the same search for perfection. The steering-wheel rim was anatomically shaped and its large boss held controls and accessories. Digital instruments were mounted in the driver's line of sight. Mechanically, the Sibilo was based on the Lancia Stratos.

1978 — Il Tempo Gigante A full-size reproduction of a model car built for use in an animated film, 'The Pinchcliffe Grand Prix', made in Norway by Ivo Caprino. 22 feet long, 8 feet wide and weighing 3 tons, the life-size version of the car carried all the equipment attributed to its imaginatively-designed model counterpart — although not all of the components, such as radar, TV cameras, anemometer, compass, barometer, altimeter, sonar, blood-bank, etc., actually worked! The engine certainly did, however.

1978-1979 — b + b Studie Cw 311
Rainer Buchmann, a custom Porsche specialist, and his collaborator Eberhard Schulz asked themselves what a Mercedes sports car of the 'eighties would look like if Daimler-Benz decided to make one. Their answer was the Cw 311, a combination of the Mercedes 300 SL and the C 111. A compact two-seater, its AMG-tuned Mercedes 6.3 litre V8 was mounted centrally. Performance levels were very high and the occupants enjoyed great comfort which was combined with excellent visibility.

1979 — Dome P2. The Japanese Dome company, who manufacture automobile accessories, showed their first prototype two-seater coupé, the Dome Zero, at the Geneva Show in 1978. A year later, visitors to the Los Angeles Auto Show saw the P2, with fibreglass bodywork reminiscent of the Lamborghini Countach. The Nissan 2.7 litre six-cylinder — as used in the Datsun 280 ZX — was mounted centrally, ahead of the rear axle, in a tubular chassis which combined components from Toyota, Subaru, and Honda. The futuristic cockpit featured digital read-outs for the instruments and electronic switches which responded to the slightest touch. 'Dome' in Japanese means 'a child's dream' so it is fitting that this car should serve to bring this collection of adults' dreams to a close.

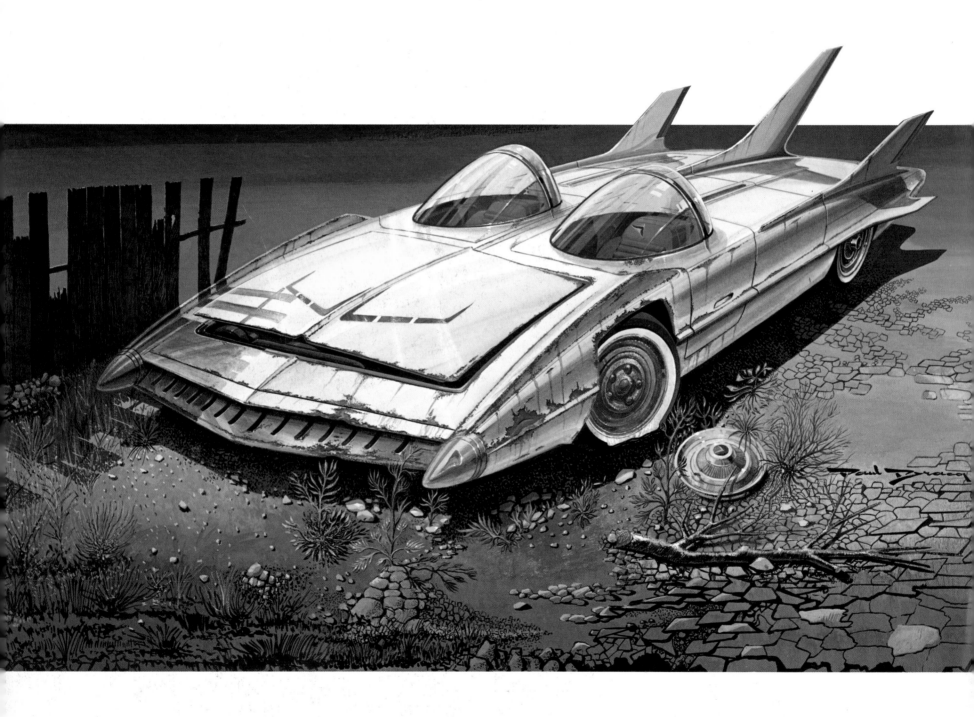

192

The dream cars' fate

Perhaps it was some immigrant Roman mythology enthusiast who named this section of the Detroit suburbs, part town and part country, Romulus, but there is little antique here. Neat bungalows with maple and birch trees in their spacious gardens, small factories on the corners where the roads cross at right-angles, an airport alongside one of the many multi-laned highways. It was these highways that had brought us here, following the numbered direction signs which corresponded with the route instructions which we had received by telephone the night before. Carefully noted down, the instructions with their road numbers and cryptic descriptions of cardinal points had seemed like a coded message—a fitting introduction to the secretive headquarters of the public relations department of Ford's Design Studio.

According to the notes, it was at the second intersection—and there it was, just as they had described it, a grey building surrounded by wire-mesh fences. The guard in the gate-house was a woman, and she asked for details of who we were and who we wished to see. The inter-com into which she spoke these details signified a tinny acceptance and we were directed to a parking-place next to the building's entrance. Once inside, we were again asked for our details and again our credentials were accepted. Somebody would show us the way. It was a mile or so, passing through rows of windowless concrete huts and past stacks of containers, rusting away gently. At one point an old Plymouth, its paintwork flaking, stood abandoned on three wheels.

In the last of the hangars we found a jumble of spare parts, a static model of Henry Ford's '999' racer, and—tucked away at the back—half a dozen cars shrouded in dust-sheets. 'We haven't kept all our experimental cars,' the man from Public Relations had said, 'but some of them are still in existence, stored at various locations within the company.' Was this the last resting-place of the only survivors of those stars of the automobile-show circuit, their wheels used to resting on the deepest of carpets rather than tarmac and their lustrous paintwork more used to the glare of multi-coloured spot-lights and the soft touch of a gorgeous model's *derrière* than the heat of the sun and the weekly slop-over of the sponge? How disappointed we were when we lifted the dusty shrouds and found only a white Thunderbird, the Fiesta Touareg, the Corrida, and the Megastar II.

Was it possible then, that these stars, like their human counterparts, slipped away into the shadows when their career in the spotlights was over, never to be seen again? It certainly seems that such is the case with the three largest American manufacturers for, as we found out, neither General Motors, Ford, or Chrysler were too interested in what happened to their dream cars when the dream was over.

Between 1938 and 1955 General Motors produced 38 experimental cars under the direction of styling chief Harley Earl. As new dream cars were introduced the old ones were put aside and returned to the divisions which had built them. Some of them were dismantled, but in 1955 almost all the 38 cars were still in existence and in good condition, being put on public display from time to time at exhibitions and new-model announcements. From 1956 to 1977, the five divisions and the central research department built a further 82 dream cars. What has become of these 120 extraordinary vehicles?

According to some sources, the majority of the cars have been scrapped—although the word in this case does not necessarily mean 'destroyed'. The examples which *were* destroyed immediately were essentially the life-size mock-ups in wood, plaster, and fibreglass, but there were not many of these. According to other opinions, the surviving cars were all parked in a warehouse near to the Design Centre and no-one was allowed to see them. This again is not completely true, for we have been able to photograph half a dozen of the dozen which GM have preserved at the Warren Technical Centre, and we have been able to do the same with the Buick Y-Job, the Buick Le Sabre, the XP300, Wildcat II, Silver Arrow I and III, the Cadillac Cyclone, the Centurion, the Chevrolet Super Spyder, Corvega, and a Corvette, together with the Pontiac Trans-Am Station Wagon which are all on display at the Alfred P. Sloan Museum at Flint.

Other rumours speak of the existence at Warren of a vast automobile cemetery where enormous sheets hide everything, including a number of experimental cars, from the gaze of the curious—even from the air. These models were supposedly destined for the breaker's torch for a number of reasons—sometimes financial—but were 'reprieved' by sympathetic employees who turned a blind eye to their instructions. We could not verify this story, but GM does admit unofficially the possibility that some of its dream cars could be in private hands.

It is surprising that only a few of GM's dream cars are still in the company's hands, but it must be remembered that many models—notably the majority of the Corvette derivatives—were modifications of the original vehicle. Once stripped of its bodywork, a chassis would often receive a new body for a new life—a process of reincarnation which was sometimes repeated more than

194

once. Nevertheless, more than half of the dream cars produced by America's most powerful automobile company no longer exist, and one can only wonder why, knowing that the reasons must be manifold.

Dream cars come from a philosophy which looks only to the future and has no place for nostalgia. Because they were often the precursors of new production models, they were automatically rendered obsolete as soon as the production models were introduced and, like the sculptor's sketches which are thrown away as soon as the work is completed, these 'sketches' too were discarded. Changes of policy and personnel helped their slide into the corporate cellars, where they were forgotten until the next clear-out. As they disappeared from sight they also had to disappear from the inventory to keep the accountants happy, so tracking them down becomes almost impossible. In the case of GM, there was never any thought of building a permanent resting place for them, even though there was no lack of space in the massive Warren research complex which the company opened in 1956. If you ask Chrysler what has happened to the 45 dream cars which they produced between 1941 and 1979, the answer is that they no longer exist, for officially they were all destroyed. The destruction policy was not as complete as the company would have us believe, however, and the proof lies in the hands of two American collectors, one of whom owns two of the six Thunderbolts built in 1941. The other is the proud possessor of one of the three Falcons built in 1955 and the 1957 Dart. They are certainly not the only people who have acquired one or more of Chrysler's 'idea cars', as the company called them, and others are believed to rest in South America, Europe, and the Middle East. The 1960 Plymouth XNR, for instance, passed into the hands of a Geneva butcher before being transferred to—it is thought— the Shah of Iran. It surfaced again in 1972 in Kuwait, according to an interview which its creator, Virgil M. Exner, gave to 'Special Interest Autos' in that same year. There is no doubt, however, about the fate of the Chrysler Norseman of 1956. Its chosen method of delivery from the Ghia factory to America was on board the ill-fated *Andrea Doria* and the car now lies in several hundred feet of water off the coast of North Carolina. Chrysler's dream cars were of particular interest to collectors because apart from one one or two exceptions, they were all fully-equipped vehicles capable of normal use.

At Ford it was different. Fifteen of the twenty 'concept cars' which the company built in the 'fifties and 'sixties were only mock-ups, often not even life-size, and there is little doubt that they were destroyed as soon as their life as exhibits was over. Some of them would not have been out of place as permanent exhibits in the Ford Museum at Dearborn, close to their birth-place in the Styling Centre. The later models, particularly those built in the Ghia workshops in Turin after their purchase by Ford in 1973 and others built in the Dearborn Styling Centre, have almost all been retained, according to the Styling Centre's P.R. department, and are exhibited from time to time.

As a general rule, American dream cars are the work of the car manufacturers, whilst in Europe they are produced by coachbuilders—more particularly the Italians. Originally, the coachbuilders were involved in the construction of one-off bodies for individual clients. With the decline of this market, they had to look for another method of drawing attention to their products and to create new contacts with the established vehicle manufacturers. By building 'prototypes' and 'design studies' for manufacturers or on their own initiative, they were able to display their abilities in the fields of creativity and craftsmanship. These lovingly constructed cars represented a series of steps along each builder's path in the search for perfection and were usually preserved, avoiding the fate which befell so many of their American counterparts.

Between 1950 and 1979, Bertone built 55 prototypes, not all of which could be described as dream cars. Fourteen of them are still in the possession of the company, the earliest being the Abarth record-car of 1956 and the Corvair Testudo of 1960. Of the remainder, some were passed over to the companies on whose behalf they were built, some sold to individuals, and some have gone to museums—the 1976 Navajo and the Carabo of 1968 are on display in the Alfa Romeo museum at Arese.

At Pininfarina, some 19 of the 40 dream cars built during the last thirty years are still kept by the company, the oldest of these being the PF X of 1960. Five cars are now in museums; the Alfa Romeo 33 of 1969 and Eagle of 1975 are on display in Italy, the PF Sigma is in Switzerland, the Fiat Y is in America, and there is the Ferrari P6 in an English museum's collection. Others went to the constructors who commissioned them, like the BMC Berlinetta, or were sold to companies abroad, like the Fiat Abarth 2000 Coupé. Since it was founded in 1968, Ital Design has made 14 dream cars, and so far as we have been able to ascertain, they all still exist, either as the property of Ital Design in Turin, or as the property of the manufacturers who made the mechanical components on which they were based.

The task of future industrial archeologists will not be an easy one for, as we have seen, the records concerning dream cars are somewhat murky. One can only wonder what the reactions of future generations would be if such archeologists of tomorrow were to disinter from their resting places these concrete examples of how their ancestors expressed their imperfect vision of the future.

196

Dream cars and prototypes: principal constructors and coachbuilders

Bertone

1950	Fiat 1900 Western Arrow cabriolet
	Ferrari cabriolet
1952	Borgward
	Abarth coupé
1953	Dodge Zeder
	Aston Martin DB2/4
	Fiat Siata 8V
	Bentley
1953-54	Alfa Romeo BAT 5-BAT 7
1955	Alfa Romeo BAT 9
1956	Abarth record
1958	Jaguar XK 140
	Ford Zodiac
1959	Maserati 3500
	Fiat Osca 1500
1960	Ferrari 250
	Gordon Peerless
1961	Ferrari 250 GT
	Maserati 5000 coupé
	Aston Martin DB 4
1962	Iso Grifo Bizzarrini
	Alfa Romeo High Speed coupé
1963	Corvair Testudo
1964	Bizzarrini coupé
	Alfa Romeo Canguro
1965	Ford Mustang
1966	Jaguar FT
	Porsche 911 Spider
1967	Jaguar Pirana
	Lamborghini Miura Spider
	Alfa Romeo Montreal
	Lamborghini Marzal
	Fiat 125 Executive
1968	Alfa Romeo Carabo
1969	BMW 2800 Spicup
	Fiat 128 coupé
	Autobianchi Runabout
1970	BMW 2002 ti Garmisch
	Chrysler Shake
	Lamborghini Urraco
	Lancia Stratos Prototipo
1971	Lamborghini Countach
1972	Suzuki Go
	Citroën Camargue
1973	NSU Trapeze
1974	Fiat 127 Village
	Lamborghini Bravo

R=dream car
S=show car, modified production model

1975	Fiat X1/9 Dallara
1976	Alfa Romeo Navajo
	Ferrari Rainbow
1977	Jaguar Ascot
1978	Lancia Sibilo
1979	Volvo Tundra

Buick-General Motors

1938	Y-Job (SO 13690)	R
1947	Y-Job (modified)	R
1950	Shooting brake	S
1951	Le Sabre roadster (XP 8, SO 9830)	R
1951	XP 300 (XP 8, SO 9864)	R
1953	Wildcat roadster (SO 1714)	R
	Le Sabre (modified)	R
1954	Wildcat II (SO 1940)	R
	Roadmaster landau (SO 1936)	S
1955	Wildcat III	R
1956	Centurion coupé (XP 301, SO 2489)	R
1957	Century cabriolet	S
1958	Wells Fargo	S
1959	XP-75 coupé 2 places	S
1961	Flamingo cabriolet	S
1962	Skylark cabriolet	S
	Skylark coupé	S
1963	W.L.M. Riviera	S
1964	Silver Arrow I Riviera	S
1968	Silver Arrow II Riviera	S
1969	Century Cruiser (ex Firebird IV)	R
1970	G.S.	S
1971	W.L.M. Riviera	S
1972	Silver Arrow III Riviera	S

Cadillac-General Motors

1933	V16 Aero Coupé (Chicago World's Fair)	S
1938	V16 Fastback (Knudsen)	S
1940	60 Special saloon 4 door (Knudsen)	S
1941	60 Special saloon 4 door (Wilson)	S
1949	60 S Embassy saloon 4 door	S
	El Rancho cabriolet	S
	Fleetwood Coupé de Ville	S

	Carribean 60 S saloon 4 door	S
1953	Le Mans roadster (SO 1709)	R
	Orleans saloon 4 door (SO 1619)	R
1954	La Espada roadster 2 seater (SO 1928)	R
	Park Avenue saloon 4 door (SO 1930)	R
	El Camino coupé 2 seater (SO 1929)	R
1955	La Salle II roadster (XP 34, SO 2220)	R
	La Salle II saloon 4 door (XP 32)	R
	Eldorado Brougham 4 door saloon (XP 38, SO 2253)	R
1956	Eldorado Brougham coupé de ville (XP 500, SO 2491)	R
1959	Cyclone roadster (XP 74, SO 90450)	R
1960	Cyclone (modified)	R
1963	Eldorado Colt cabriolet	S
1964	Florentine coupé	S
1967	W.L.M. Eldorado	S
1968	El Dorado Biarritz coupé de ville	S
1971	El Dorado cabriolet	S
1972	Blue Boy, El Dorado cabriolet	S
1975	Seville Elegante	S

Chevrolet-General Motors

1953	Corvette roadster (SO 1737)	R
1954	Corvette Nomad station wagon (SO 1954)	R
	Corvette Corvair coupé 2 door (SO 2071)	R
	Corvette coupé hardtop (SO 2000)	S
1955	Biscayne 4 door hardtop (XP 37)	R
1956	Impala coupé 2 door (XP 100, SO 2487)	R
	Corvette SR 2 first version	S
	Corvette SR 2 second version	S

Year	Model	
	Corvette SS (New York Show)	S
1957	Corvette SS, Sebring Race (XP 64, SO 90158)	R
	Corvette SR 2 Daytona third version	S
	Corvette SR 2 fourth version	S
1958	Corvette XP 700 (SO 90368)	R
1959	Stingray roadster (XP 87)	R
1960	Corvette XP 700 (modified)	R
	Corvette CERV 1 single seater	S
	Corvair Spyder cabriolet 2 seater	R
1961	Stingray roadster (modified)	R
	Corvair Sebring Spyder (XP 737, SO 90832)	S
1962	Stingray roadster (modified)	R
	Corvette Shark (XP 755, SO 90918)	S
	Corvair Monza GT coupé (XP 777, SO 91117)	R
1963	Corvette Stingray cabriolet	S
	Corvair Super Spyder (XP 785, SO 91033)	S
	Corvair Monza SS roadster (XP 797, SO 91246)	R
1964	Corvette Stingray coupé	S
	Super Nova coupé 2 door (SO 828)	S
1965	Mako Shark II (1/1 scale model) (XP 830, SO 10424)	R
	Caribe cabriolet 4 door (XP 834, SO 19000)	S
1966	Corvette Mako Shark II	R
	Stingray roadster (modified)	S
1967	Astro 1 coupé (XP 842, SO 19019)	R
1968	Astro-Vette roadster	S
	Astro II mid-engined coupé first version (XP 880)	R
1969	Corvette Aero coupé	S
	Corvette Shark I (modified)	R
	Corvette Manta Ray (ex Mako Shark II)	S
	Astro III, 3-wheel turbine car	R
1970	Astro mid-engined second version (XP 880)	R
	Camaro ZL-1 coupé	S
1971	Corvega coupé 2 door	S
1972	Camaro Berlinetta	S
1973	Corvette Sirocco	S
	Corvette Wankel 2 rotor engine	R
	Corvette Wankel 4 rotor Aero-Vette	R
	Coupé 2 door (XP 898)	R
	Monza coupé (prototype)	R
1974	Corvette Mulsanne (ex Sirocco)	S
1975	Super Monza coupé 2+2	S

Chrysler

Year	Model	
1940	Thunderbolt roadster (Le Baron)	R
	Newport phaeton (Le Baron)	R
1950	Plymouth XX-500 (Ghia)	R
1951	Chrysler K-310 coupé (Ghia)	R
1952	Chrysler C-200 cabriolet (Ghia)	R
	Chrysler Special coupé fastback (Ghia)	R
1953	Chrysler Special modified (Ghia)	S
	Chrysler GS-1 tiny production run (Ghia)	
	Chrysler D'Elégance (Ghia)	R
	Dodge Firearrow I (1/1 scale model) Ghia	R
1954	Plymouth Belmont (Briggs Manufacturing)	R
	Plymouth Explorer coupé (Ghia)	R
	De Soto Adventurer I coupé (Ghia)	R
	Dodge Firearrow II roadster (Ghia)	R
	Dodge Firearrow III coupé (Ghia)	R
	Dodge Firearrow IV cabriolet (Ghia)	R
	De Soto Adventurer II coupé (Ghia)	R
1955	Dodge Granada (Briggs Manufacturing)	R
	Falcon roadster (Ghia)	R
	Flight-Sweep I cabriolet (Ghia)	R
	Flight-Sweep II cabriolet (Ghia)	R
1956	Plainsman station wagon (Ghia)	R
	Norseman coupé fastback (Ghia)	R
1957	Chrysler Dart (Ghia)	R
1958	Plymouth Cabana station wagon (1/1 scale model) (Ghia)	R
	Imperial D'Elégance (1/1 scale model)	R
1959	De Soto Cella I (3/8 scale model)	R
1960	Plymouth XNR (Ghia)	R
1961	Dodge Flitewing (Ghia)	R
	Chrysler Turboflite (Ghia)	R
1963	Chrysler Turbine	
	Plymouth Satellite	S
1965	Plymouth VIP	S
	Dodge Charger II	R
1967	Chrysler 300X	R
1969	Chrysler Concept 70 X	R
	Plymouth Duster I	R
1970	Dodge Charger III	R
1979	Cordoba d'Oro	R

Ford

1953	Lincoln-Mercury XL-500
	Ford X-100
1954	Ford FX-Atmos
	Lincoln-Mercury Monterey XM-800
1955	Ford X-500
	Lincoln Futura
1956	Mercury Turnpike Cruiser (Ghia)
	Ford Roof-O-Matic
	Ford Mystère
	Ford X-1000
1958	Ford La Galaxie
	Ford Glideair
	Ford Nucleon
	Ford X-2000
1959	Ford La Tosca
	Ford Levacar
1961	Ford Gyron
	Ford Volante
1962	Ford Cougar 404
	Ford Seattle-ite XXI
1963	Ford Allegro
	Ford Cougar II
	Ford Mustang II
	Lincoln-Mercury Super Cyclone
	Mercury Montego
	Mercury Super Marauder
1964	Lincoln-Mercury Park Lane 400
	Ford Aurora
1965	Lincoln-Mercury Mercury Astron
	Mercury Comet Escapade
	Mercury Comet Cyclone Sportster
	Lincoln Continental Coronation Coupe
	Ford Black Pearl
1969	Ford Super Cobra
	Mercury Super Spoiler
	Ford Mark II Dual Cowl Phaeton
1970	Ford Tridon
1974	Ford Coins (Ghia)
1977	Ford Corrida (Ghia)
	Ford Megastar I (Ghia)
1978	Ford Megastar II (Ghia)
	Ford Microsport (Ghia)
	Ford Action (Ghia)
1979	Ford Navarre (Ghia)
	Ford Lucano (Ghia)
	Ford Probe 1

General Motors

Year	Model	
1954	Firebird I, turbine car (XP 21, SO 1921)	R

1956	Firebird II, turbine car (XP 43, SO 2683)	R
1956	Free piston project XP 500	R
1958	Firebird III, turbine car (XP 73, SO 90238)	R
1964	Firebird IV, turbine car (XP 790, SO 91331)	R
	GMX Stiletto (XP 759, SO 91383)	R
	Runabout, 3 wheeler (XP 792, SO 91327)	R
1968	Aero-Coupe, retractable roof (XP 856)	R
1969	GM Commuters Delta 511	R
1972	Hybrid, electric car	R

General Motors-Associates

| 1969 | Opel CD | R |
| 1970 | SRV Vauxhall | R |

Ghia

1951	Plymouth XX-500 (Chrysler)
1951	Chrysler K-310 coupé (Chrysler)
1952	Chrysler C-200 cabriolet (Chrysler)
	Chrysler Special fastback coupé (Chrysler)
1953	Chrysler Special new version (Chrysler)
	De Soto Adventurer I coupé (Chrysler)
	Chrysler GS-1 (short run production for Chrysler France)
	Dodge Firearrow I roadster (Chrysler)
	Chrysler d'Elegance (Chrysler)
1954	Plymouth Explorer coupé (Chrysler)
	Dodge Firearrow II roadster (Chrysler)
	Dodge Firearrow III coupé (Chrysler)
	Dodge Firearrow IV cabriolet (Chrysler)
	De Soto Adventurer II coupé (Chrysler)
1955	Gilda or Streamline
	Falcon roadster (Chrysler)
	Flight-Sweep I cabriolet (Chrysler)
	Flight-Sweep II cabriolet (Chrysler)
1956	Ferrari 410 Superamerica coupé
	Plainsman station wagon (Chrysler)
	Norseman fastback coupé (Chrysler)
1957	Dart (Chrysler)
1958	Plymouth Cabana station wagon (Chrysler)

1959	Imperial D'Elégance (Chrysler)
1959	Selene I
1960	Plymouth XNR roadster (Chrysler)
1961	Dodge Flitewing (Chrysler)
	Turbo Flite (Chrysler)
1962	Selene II
1965	Bugatti 101-C
1966	De Tomaso Mangusta
1968	De Tomaso Mangusta Spyder
1970	De Tomaso Pantera
1971	Zonda
1974	Coins (Ford)
1977	Corrida (Ford)
	Megastar I (Ford)
1978	Megastar II (Ford)
	Microsport (Ford)
	Action (Ford)
1979	Navarre (Ford)
	Lucano (Ford)

Ital Design

1968	Manta Bizzarini
1969	Alfa Romeo Iguana
	Abarth 1600
1970	Volkswagen Porsche Tapiro
1971	Volkswagen Karmann Cheetah
	Alfasud Caimano
1972	Maserati Boomerang
1973	Audi As de Pique
1974	Maserati coupé
1976	Medici II
	BMW Karmann As de Carreau
1978	Lancia Megagamma

Oldsmobile-General Motors

1953	Starfire (XP 200, SO 1621)	R
1954	F-88 (XP 20, SO 1939)	R
	Cutlass (SO 1981)	R
1955	88 Delta coupé 2 door (XP 40, SO 2251)	R
1956	Golden Rocket coupé 2 door (XP 400, SO 2490)	R
1957	F-88 Mark II cabriolet 2 seater	R
1959	F-88 Mark III cabriolet 2 seater (XP 88, SO 90388)	R
1962	F85 roadster	S
1964	El Torero 98 cabriolet	S
1968	Toronado Gran Turismo 2 seater (XP 866)	S
1973	Toronado XSR	S

Pininfarina

1936	Lancia Aprilia aerodynamic coupé
1952	Lancia Aurelia PF
1956	Alfa Romeo Super Flow I
1959	Cadillac Starlight

1960	PF 'X'
1961	PF 'Y'
	Cadillac 'Jacqueline'
1962	Chevrolet Corvair coupé
1963	Chevrolet Corvette Rondine
	PF Sigma
1965	Fiat Abarth special coupé
	Alfa Romeo Giulia Sport special coupé
1966	Dino Berlinetta GT
1967	Dino competition
	Ferrari 365 P Berlinetta Spéciale
	BMC aerodynamic saloon
1968	Fiat Dino Geneva
	BLMC aerodynamic saloon
	Alfa Romeo P/33
	Ferrari 250/P5
	Ferrari P6
1969	Sigma Grand Prix
	Ferrari 512 S
	Alfa Romeo 33
	Fiat Abarth 2000 special coupé
1970	PF Modulo
1971	NSU Ro 80
	Ferrari BB
1972	Alfa Romeo Alfetta Spider
1973	Autobianchi All2 Giovani
	Jaguar XJ 12
1974	Abarth SE 030
	Studio Cr 25
1975	Alfa Romeo Eagle
1978	Ideal Aerodynamic Form
1978-79	Jaguar Spider XJ 12

Pontiac-General Motors

1953	Parisienne Landau (SO 1759)	S
1954	Strato Streak 4 door hardtop (SO 1953)	R
	Bonneville Special coupé 2 door (SO 2026)	R
1955	Strato Star coupé 2 door (XP 36)	R
1956	Club de Mer roadster (XP 200, SO 2488)	R
1962	XP 400 cabriolet	S
	Tempest Monte Carlo roadster (XP 741, SO 90874)	S
1963	Banshee 2 seater coupé (XP 758)	R
	Bonneville Maharani cabriolet	S
	Tempest Fleur de Lis	S
1964	X400 cabriolet (XP 826)	S
1968	Firebird roadster	R
1969	Cirrus (ex 1964 GMX)	R
	Fiero (ex Firebird roadster)	S
1970	Firebird Black Knight	S
1972	Firebird Pegasus	S
1973	Banshee coupé 2 door	S
	Phantom	R
1974	Firebird Pegasus (modified)	S

Dream cars
in miniature

Model	Maker	Scale	Material
Abarth 2000	ST	1/24	PK
Prototype Pininfarina	Nakamura	1/24	PK
	Marushi	1/43	M
	Gama	1/43	M
Alfa Romeo	Dinky-Toys	1/43	M
Carabo Bertone	Lesney	1/43	M
	Mercury	1/43	M
	Politoys	1/25	M
	Solido	1/43	M
	Togi	1/23	MK
Alfa Romeo	Meteboys	1/43	M
Iguana Ital Design	Politoys	1/43	M
Alfa Romeo P/33	Mercury	1/43	M
Pininfarina			
Autobianchi	Lesney	1/50	M
Runabout Bertone	Meteboys	1/43	M
	Meccano Triang	1/18	P
Bizzarrini Manta	Mercury	1/43	M
Ital Design			
BMC 1800 Pininfarina	Lesney	1/43	M
BMW Turbo	Crown	1/24	PK
	Norev	1/43	M
	Nakamura	1/24	PK
	Marushin	1/43	M
	Schuco	1/43	M
	Schuco	1/16	P
Chevrolet Astro I	Pilen	1/43	M
	AMT	1/25	PK
Chevrolet Astro-Vette	MPC	1/25	PK
Chevrolet Corvair	Aurora	1/32	PK
Monza SS			
Chevrolet Corvair	Palmer	1/24	PK
Monza GT	Aurora	1/32	PK
	Edai-Grip	1/20	PK

Model	Maker	Scale	Material
Chevrolet Corvette	Monogram	1/24	MPK
1953	AMT	1/25	PK
	Milestone	1/43	M
Chevrolet Corvette	MPC	1/25	PK
Mako Shark II	Gosen	1/24	PK
Chevrolet Corvette	Lindbergh	1/18	PK
4-Rotor			
Chevrolet Corvette	Classic Car	1/43	MK
SS Sebring			
Chrysler Turbine Car	Jo-Han	1/25	PK
Citroën Camargue	Norev	1/43	M
Bertone			
De Tomaso	Dinky-Toys	1/43	M
Mangusta Ghia	Politoys	1/25	M
	Solido	1/43	M
	Bandai	1/20	PK
De Tomaso	Politoys	1/43	M
Pantera Ghia	Nitto	1/26	PK
	Norev	1/43	M
	Heller	1/25	PK
	Aoshima	1/20	PK
	Imai	1/24	PK
	Marui	1/24	PK
	Nichimo	1/25	PK
Dome-O	Fujimi	1/24	PK
	Kado	1/43	M
Dino Berlinetta	Nitto	1/24	PK
Competizione	Nitto	1/28	PK
Pininfarina	Marashin	1/43	M
Ferrari Dino	Politoys	1/43	M
Berlinetta Pininfarina			
Ferrari 512/S	Politoys	1/43	M
Pininfarina	Norev	1/43	M
	Pilen	1/43	M

Model	Maker	Scale	Material
Ferrari Modulo	Mercury	1/32	M
Pininfarina	Politoys	1/43	M
	Pilen	1/43	M
Ferrari Rainbow	Edai-Grip	1/24	PK
Bertone	Grip	1/43	M
Ferrari 250 P/5	Pilen	1/43	M
Berlinetta Speciale	Polistil	1/43	M
Pininfarina	Aurora	1/25	PK
	Apollo	1/20	PK
Fiat Turbine	ABC	1/43	P
Jaguar Pirana	Otaki	1/16	PK
Bertone	Polistil	1/43	M
Lancia Stratos	Pilen	1/43	M
Prototipo Bertone			
Lamborghini	Arii	1/20	PK
Countach Bertone	Aoshima	1/16	PK
	Aoshima	1/20	PK
	Edai-Grip	1/24	PK
	Fujimi	1/16	PK
	Imai	1/24	PK
	Marui	1/24	PK
	Nichimo	1/24	PK
	Nitto	1/24	PK
	Nitto	1/28	PK
	Otaki	1/12	PK
	Tamiya	1/24	PK
	Grip-Technica	1/28	M
	Sakura	1/43	M
	Marushin	1/43	M
	ST HO	1/87	MK
	Diapet	1/43	M
	Sakamura	1/43	M
	Grip	1/20	PK
Lamborghini Marzal	Dinky-Toys	1/43	M
Bertone	Lesney	1/43	M
	Politoys	1/43	M

Model	Maker	Scale	Material
Lamborghini Marzal	AHM	1/20	PK
Bertone	Bandai	1/20	PK
	Monogram	1/24	PK
	Polistil	1/43	M
Lamborghini Urraco	Meteboys	1/43	M
Bertone	Politoys	1/43	M
	LS	1/24	PK
Lincoln Futura	Revell	1/25	PK
Maserati Boomerang	Siku	1/66	M
Ital Design	Aoshima	1/16	PK
	Aoshima	1/20	PK
	Edai-Grip	1/24	PK
	Grip	1/43	M
	ST HO	1/87	MK
Mercedes-Benz C 111	Corgi Toys	1/43	M
	Dinky-Toys	1/43	M
	Lesney	1/50	M
	Märklin	1/43	M
	Meteboys	1/43	M
	Mercury	1/43	M
	Norev	1/43	P
	Norev	1/43	M
	Schuco	1/18	P
	Solido	1/43	M
	Crown	1/24	PK
	Gama	1/43	M
	Wiking	1/87	P
	Nakamura	1/24	PK
	Polistil	1/43	M
	Pilen	1/43	M
Mercer Cobra	Renwal	1/25	PK
Panther Bertone	Mercury	1/43	M
	Edai-Grip	1/20	PK
PF X Pininfarina	Mercury	1/43	M
Pontiac Club de Mer	Revell	1/25	PK

P = plastic   M = metal   K = kit

Works consulted

Great Automobile Designs, John McIellan — Arco Publishing Company 1975.

Buick: The Postwar Years, Jan P. Norbye & Jim Dunne — Motorbooks International 1978.

The Complete Book of Automobile Body Design, Ian Beattie — Haynes 1977.

Style Auto Architettura della Carrozzeria 4, 7, 8, 13.

The Real Corvette, an illustrated history of Chevrolet's sports car, Ray Miller — The Evergreen Press 1975.

Cars of the Stars, George Barris & Jack Scagnetti — Jonathan David Publishers 1974.

Chrome Dreams, automobile styling since 1893, Paul C. Wilson — Chilton Book Co. 1976.

Chevy/Corvette Portfolio — Performance Media 1975.

Corvette, the complete history, Karl Ludvigsen — Automobile Quarterly Publications 1978.

Cadillac, the complete history, Maurice D. Hendry — Automobile Quarterly Publications 1979.

Sixty Years of Chevrolet, George H. Dammann — Crestline Publishing 1972.

Famous Custom and Show Cars, George Barris & Jack Scagnetti — E. P. Dutton 1973.

Special-Interest Autos magazines.

L'Année Automobile / Automobile Year — Edita S.A. 1953-1979.

My Years with General Motors, Alfred P. Sloan Jr. — Doubleday & Co. 1964.

Seventy Years of Buick, George H. Dammann — Cretline Publishing 1973.

Automobiles of America — Wayne State University Press 1968.

Automobile Quarterly 8/4, 13/1 — Automobile Quarterly.

Chrysler and Imperial, the postwar years, Richard M. Langworth — Motorbooks International 1976.

Carrozzeria Italiana, cultura e progetto — Alfieri 1978.

L'auto è femmina, vent'anni di stile carrozzerio a Torino — Motor Italia 1968.

Car Styling Special Number 19 Bertone — Car Styling 1977.

Car Styling Special Edition 23 Luigi Colani: Designing Tomorrow — Car Styling 1979.

Dino, the little Ferrari, Doug Nye — Osprey Publishing Limited 1979.

Pininfarina, 1930-1980, Prestige and Tradition, Didier Merlin— Edita S.A. 1980.

Catalogues de la Revue Automobile 1952-1980.

Acknowledgements

The author wishes to extend his warmest thanks to all those persons, firms, institutions and museums who have given him precious help in the preparation of this book, and in particular: MM. Takeo Arai, Nissan Motor; George Barris, Barris Kustom Industries; Nuccio Bertone; Eugene Bordinat, Ford Motor Company: Paul Bracq. Centre Style Peugeot: William M. Brownlie, Chrysler Corporation; Ivo Caprino; Bill Carroll, Ford Motor Company: Mrs Billie Delevich, General Motors Corporation: MM. Yoshitada Fujimaki, Toyota Motor; Akira Fujimoto, Car Styling; Akira Fujino, Daihatsu Motor; Giorgio Giugiaro; Tony Hogg, Road & Track; Dave Holls, General Motors Corporation; Takeshi Ichinashi, Isuzu Motors; E.P. Jacoby, Chrysler Corporation: Tom Jakobowski, Chrysler Corporation: Shotaro Kobayashi, Car Graphic; Phillip C. Kwiatkowski, Alfred P. Sloan Jr. Museum; R.G. Macadam, Chrysler Corporation; John F. Maciarz, General Motors Corporation; William L. Mitchell; Giuliano Molineri, Ital Design SIRP; A. Molteni, Carrozzeria Pininfarina; Pierre Ollier, General Motors Corporation; G.B. Panicco, Carrozzeria Bertone; Sergio Pininfarina; Irvin W. Rybicki, General Motors Corporation; Filippo Sapino, Ghia; Dick H. Strassl, BMW; Shoji Tabuko, Toyo Kogyo; Fredi Valentini, Carrozzeria Pininfarina; Jean-Claude Villard, General Motors Suisse; T. Yukawa, Nissan Motor; R.F. Zokas, Ford Motor Company; and Dominique Gross, faithful companion in his American wanderings.

Photographic Credits

Photolithography Actual, Bienne
Printed by GEA, Milan
Bound by Maurice Busenhart S.A., Lausanne

Printed in Italy